BIGFOOT

Photo © Rachel Pardo/Olan Mills

Tom Burnette is a native of the North Carolina Smoky Mountains, adjacent to Pisgah National Park. He earned a Bachelor of Science degree from Georgia College with minors in biology and geology. Tom is a real estate investor and trains lifeguards for a living. In 1999 he self-published his controversial book, *Nature's Secret Agents.* He has also been a regular guest on such radio shows as *Let's Talk Paranormal*, *Bigfoot Lives*, and *Sasquatch Watch* online radio.

Photo © Ashley Petershagen

Rob Riggs is a native of Sour Lake, a small town in the Big Thicket region of Southeast Texas. He studied philosophy and literature at the University of Texas at Austin and holds a Bachelor of Arts degree in the prestigious Plan II Liberal Arts honors program. Rob is a twenty-five-year veteran journalist and has two successful books: *In the Big Thicket: On the Trail of the Wild Man* and (as coauthor) *Weird Texas: Your Travel Guide to Texas's Local Legends and Best Kept Secrets.*

EXPLORING THE MYTH & DISCOVERING THE TRUTH

BIGFOOT

TOM BURNETTE
& ROB RIGGS

Llewellyn Publications

Woodbury, Minnesota

First Edition
First Printing, 2014

Book design by Bob Gaul
Cover design by Kevin R. Brown
Cover illustration by Dominick Finelle/The July Group
Interior photo by Tom Burnette

Llewellyn Publications is a registered trademark of Llewellyn Worldwide Ltd.

Library of Congress Cataloging-in-Publication Data
Burnette, Tom.
  Bigfoot: exploring the myth & discovering the truth/by Tom Burnette and Rob Riggs.—First edition.
    pages cm
  ISBN 978-0-7387-3631-0
  1. Sasquatch. I. Riggs, Rob. II. Title.
  QL89.2.S2B874 2014
  001.944—dc23
                        2013037367

Llewellyn Publications
A Division of Llewellyn Worldwide Ltd.
2143 Wooddale Drive
Woodbury, MN 55125-2989
www.llewellyn.com

Printed in the United States of America

CONTENTS

INTRODUCTION

This book is based on Tom Burnette's and Rob Riggs's many years of investigations of an unknown and peculiarly elusive animal—and on interviews of eyewitnesses of apparently the same cryptic beast—conducted during our twenty-plus years each of field research.

Bigfoot is admittedly a loaded word. For most people it evokes a knee-jerk reaction. Either they already believe in the existence of an undiscovered hairy ape/man or they don't. If they don't, that's usually the end of the discussion. Even if they do believe, they likely will have a set of assumptions, which could range anywhere from its being a brutish ape to a telepathic superhuman, and will only be looking only at the evidence consistent with their beliefs. Except for very few who claim to have had direct encounters, most people's opinions rest solely on their preconceptions. Since the supposed animal in question has never been caught, it is not clear whether people are even believing or not believing in the same thing. So, forget the word; try to forget what you already believe; you just might find this material to be eye-opening.

Whether it is called Bigfoot, wild man, mystery hominid, or by a name as corny and colloquial as swamp devil or booger—this book presents evidence that an unknown big, hairy, stinky, loud, and perhaps wildly dangerous *something* inhabits the deep woods of large parts of the southern United States. Over the years, we have been subjected to considerable ridicule and inbred redneck jokes for making the claims presented in this book. Both the witnesses interviewed and we ourselves have been dismissed as superstitious and uneducated country bumpkins who are obviously deluded by wishful thinking or by the misidentification of known wildlife.

Apparently it does not occur to such critics, who invariably consider themselves to be highly urbane and sophisticated, that Bigfoot are naturally going to be seen in remote places. If they are real animals inhabiting sparsely populated parts of this country, is it not reasonable they should be seen in the backwoods of East Texas, the mountains of North Carolina, the bayous of Louisiana, the hills of Arkansas, and the swamps of Florida—not in the lecture halls of universities or rummaging through shopping mall dumpsters in cookie-cutter subdivisions?

We do not claim this is the same animal better known to make appearances in the Pacific Northwest. After considering this text, you may judge that issue for yourself. For convenience's sake, however, we will refer to the creature in question as Bigfoot. The information provided here would lead to the conclusion it is likely to be a heretofore unknown quadruped primate, but that certainly does not close the matter, nor is the mystery solved. It simply raises further questions of how a large primate could remain so elusive to official discovery, and what capabilities it might have to enable it to stay hidden.

So what qualifies a couple of southern country boys to expound on the subject of Bigfoot and its attendant issues? To begin with, this is not our first rodeo. In addition to various newspaper and magazine articles and interviews by each of us, both of us have had prior books published. Tom is the author of *Nature's Secret Agent* published in 1999, and Rob wrote *In the Big Thicket: On the Trail of the Wild Man*, which came out in 2001.

Both of us conducted many years of separate field research, during which we were totally unknown to one another, only to eventually learn our respective findings firmly corroborate one another down to highly specific details unrecorded elsewhere. These include our independent respective discoveries of bizarre energy and light-form manifestations—documented with photographs by both of us—which are apparently concurrent with Bigfoot sightings. They suggest that we are, indeed, dealing with a physically real being, but it might be even stranger than we had imagined. In part, this is the story of how we came to collaborate in our research and on this book after having individually made these observations.

Neither of us set out in life wanting to be a Bigfoot researcher or to write books about Bigfoot. However, both of us found ourselves in circumstances that compelled us to investigate stories of unknown, ape-like creatures. Sightings of the creatures had been reported for many years in the rural southern backwoods areas where we grew up, Tom in the Smoky Mountains of western North Carolina, and Rob in the swamplands of the Big Thicket in Southeast Texas.

The parts of the text written in narrative form should be taken as both of us speaking. Where our individual views and respective research projects and experiences are presented they will be noted as such, and each of us will either be cited or directly quoted as required.

Our Goal for the Book

There is nothing we could write, no legend we could tell, no sighting we could report and no photo we could present which in and of itself would convince anyone Bigfoot is real. We know that, but the body of evidence detailed in this book speaks for itself.

It is not our goal to shoot or capture a specimen just to prove Bigfoot exists. What we hope to do is gather enough evidence for their existence—using our own original approach to research—to raise awareness of the need to preserve these rare creatures and their fast-vanishing wild habitats.

We are dedicated to working toward Bigfoot being recognized as flesh-and-blood living beings so they can be protected from hunters and others who would exploit them. Beyond that, we are both convinced a prolonged study of these splendid creatures in their natural environment has the potential to teach humankind profound lessons about nature and the human potential.

One immediate goal is to narrow the range of the shaggy beasts' activities, to shrink the research area to be monitored, and thereby increase the odds of having enough repeated close encounters to obtain multiple conclusive photographs. The ultimate aim would be to get the Bigfoot so accustomed to a continued human presence that it would be possible to do a prolonged video-documented observation of their behavior, which would finally be accepted as concrete scientific evidence.

For this to be accomplished, someone would have to lay the groundwork by actually living in a remote area the animals also permanently inhabit or frequently visit to learn their habits, and to so accustom them to his presence as to win their trust, or at least not be considered a threat. This will not be easy, not only because the animals are so elusive and wary of human contact, but also because they are highly territorial and can be overwhelmingly intimidating and aggressive toward anyone they consider an intruder. Because of his unique circumstances, Tom Burnette might actually be well on the way to accomplishing this complex task.

Tom has experienced repeated and sometimes horrifying encounters for over two decades. Occasionally he has seen huge, black, hairy blurs of an unidentified animal running through the woods, and many times he has heard them howling, throwing around large tree limbs like they were sofa pillows, and otherwise raising an ungodly loud ruckus. He has had rocks the size of baseballs mysteriously propelled at him from the woods, with an accompanying deep guttural growl, only to land at his feet, and been left to wonder whether they could just as easily have crushed his chest or skull.

There is little doubt an ever-increasing number of field researchers and unintentional witnesses are having such horrific Bigfoot experiences. Tom Burnette is unique in having stayed in one specific area after so many encounters. Most sell out lock, stock, and barrel after their first experience, and want nothing more to do with the beasts. Many are so traumatized they cannot even bring themselves to think of what happened to them, much less speak to others about it.

Most of Tom's neighbors refuse to stay in the nearby high mountain peaks because they have had some sort of unexplainable experience of their own with the shaggy monstrosities and are afraid of them. Only an insatiable curiosity and a deep thirst for knowledge have kept Tom on his land continuing to encourage interaction with the creatures while going completely unarmed. In Rob's opinion this makes Tom a bona fide badass, but his opinion of himself is far more modest:

> I don't mind telling you, these creatures have
> scared the shit out of me a number of times. I am a
> certified Aikido and weapons expert and I remain,
> respectfully, very much afraid of them. If they want
> you, they are going to get you and there is nothing
> you can do about it. Several times they have showed
> me personally how easily they can get on top of
> you in just a few seconds, seemingly coming from
> nowhere out of the woods. They're like the Special
> Forces; now you see them and now you don't. They
> definitely have my respect. I think the work I have
> done with them over the past twenty years has
> somehow won their trust and made them respect
> me. At least they've quit eating my dogs.

His long-term efforts at considerable personal expense and risk have made an incredible contribution to research. The story of his experiences, observations, and experiments, along with some amazing photographic images he has captured, uniquely qualify him to coauthor this work. Perhaps the most intriguing of his photos (featured below) obtained with a game trail motion-sensitive camera in the summer of 2010 is what might be a full frontal shot of an unidentified quadruped hairy primate.

Photo taken by Tom Burnette

From a distance, a Bigfoot might be mistaken for a bear, but not up close. A key difference is hair texture. The Bigfoot's hair is longer and appears to have been groomed. Grooming of one another is characteristic and commonplace among monkeys and apes. His hair appears to have been manicured whereas bears in the same area are mangy looking.

As is the case with most videos and still shots of alleged Bigfoot, cynics will argue this picture is inconclusive at best. Some might even say it is more likely the rear end of a black bear. This would not account, however, for the eyes, the eyebrows, the outline of a beard, and the faint facial features that appear in what would correspond with the shoulder blades of a bear seen from the rear.

Tom is willing to undergo a lie-detector test to verify he has not tampered with the image, and we would venture to say if a wildlife expert were to closely examine the photo, there is no way a black bear could contort itself in such a way as to result in the proportions of the animal in the photo. Bears simply do not have backs that narrow or backbones and shoulder blades that protrude to such a degree.

We do not claim this photo to be definitive proof of the existence of unknown hairy primates, but when viewed within the context of the details of how it was taken and the history of sightings in the general area, it emphatically shows more investigation is justified.

Another image is equally compelling. The photo was retrieved from Tom's game trail camera on February 4, 2013, and can be seen exclusively (along with many other photos) on our website, Bigfootthebigpicture.net. It took Tom three years to get this picture, and it was one out of 7,213 photos taken. The rest were discarded. We believe this to be a juvenile Bigfoot, because of the lack of hair on the face and the smaller size compared to others we have seen but not photographed. The camera was exactly five feet off the ground, so the Bigfoot would probably be stretching to look into the camera. The younger Bigfoot appear to be curious about everything. However, since Tom's first good picture of the large male, he has never gotten another picture of him. They are well aware of anything electrical, and they seem to stay away from a functioning camera at all costs. They will turn a camera over in the mud if it is not properly fastened to a tree.

When we first looked at this photo, it occurred to us some might think it looks like the face of a barn owl or barred owl. However, there was no branch for it to have been perched on, and the camera's shutter speed was too slow to capture such a clear image had it been a moving owl. Upon closer examination, we realized the eyes are recessed into the head and there is a bony structure encircling the eyes. The face is flat, there is a nose bridge between the eyes, and the nostrils are visible, but there is no snout. All of these are distinctly primate characteristics that could not be confused with an owl or any other mammal.

Our book can be taken in part as a call for research based on Tom's groundwork that employs very specific original strategies in a highly focused geographic area, which has resulted in his having obtained these photographs and shows promise of being able to duplicate this evidence by producing more images. It is also an invitation to join us in exploring the connection we have both noted with mysterious energy fields and light-forms.

A detailed discussion of this energy connection and its implications constitutes much of Rob's contribution to this book and hopefully connects the dots to show our readers the big picture regarding the significance of the Bigfoot phenomenon. It includes considerations of relevant data from other mystery primate researchers both in this country and in Russia, and reflections on such topics as telepathy among animals, the mechanisms of human perception, and the understanding of earth energies among ancient and traditional peoples—all of which might have a bearing on the creature's confounding elusiveness and its mysterious origin.

Recent years have seen public interest in Bigfoot and related mystery creatures reach perhaps an all-time peak. This is substantiated not only by a proliferation of new books on the subject, but also by considerable attention from cable television. Several episodes of the series *Monster Quest* on History Channel have dealt with the phenomenon in various places around the country. There have also been some excellent single-episode documentaries, including *Sasquatch: Legend Meets Science,* on National Geographic Channel, *Bigfootville* on Travel Channel, and *Bigfoot: the Definitive Guide,* on History Channel. Most recently a new series, *Finding Bigfoot,* featuring the work of the BFRO began airing on Animal Planet network in 2011.

All of these programs are promising in that they all conclude there is a preponderance of evidence to suggest Bigfoot is a real live undiscovered animal. Unfortunately, they all also have in common the employment of the hit-and-miss, invade-and-conquer strategy that has proven to be unsuccessful in getting conclusive results. This might be a built-in limitation of media involvement, but in any case, it is a tactic we hope to avoid.

If you are a hardcore Bigfoot aficionado and have already read some of the many excellent books published on the subject, you should enjoy this book, as should more casual fans who have been intrigued by the well-produced TV shows mentioned above. You will likely find our original insights into the mystery to be enjoyable as they unfold, and you also will have the satisfaction of knowing that by buying our book you are supporting potential breakthrough field research into an age-old enigma.

Moreover, if you have had sightings or other experiences that have drawn you into your own quest for answers to the Bigfoot mystery, and would like to join us, we would love to hear from you. For more photos, visit Bigfootthebigpicture.net.

Rob Riggs, Sour Lake, TX
crriggs@yahoo.com

Tom Burnette, Old Fort, NC
tomburnette@hotmail.com

ONE

Bigfoot History
in Western North Carolina
and Southeastern Texas

For those who have had any kind of Bigfoot encounter, it was probably the shock of their lives. Some people who have chanced upon them in the woods have been terrified by the creatures' unbelievably loud howling. Others have stumbled across their tracks or found the ravaged remains of large animals the creatures had apparently slaughtered. Startled, unsuspecting witnesses have reported driving past them alongside remote country roads. Others have been attacked while in the presumed safety of their cars by howling, hairy monsters that jumped on the hoods and glared menacingly at them through the windshields.

Giant, ape-like beasts with glowing eyes have terrorized folks living on the edge of the woods by banging on the walls of their houses and peeking through the windows. They have been seen feasting on a variety of livestock, ranging from making munchies of penned-up chickens and rabbits to gutting and hauling off two-hundred-pound hogs. Many campers and hikers have been chased out of the woods with the hair on the back of their necks sticking straight up from the terror of feeling that the things were tracking them, or they have been scared off and sickened by the horrible putrid odor the animals emit.

With rare exceptions, these encounters are totally unexpected and happen by chance, not as a result of anyone's research efforts. Most of the time they are also life changing and leave startled eyewitnesses fearful of ridicule and disbelief if they speak of their experiences. Worse yet, sometimes these witnesses are left questioning their own sanity.

Our experience is that more sightings come from hunters, fishermen, campers, and outdoors enthusiasts than from any other source. Their accounts also usually contain the most descriptive detail. If Bigfoot is a real animal that inhabits remote forested areas of this country, then it makes sense most sightings come from people who spend the most time in the woods. This fact is one good argument for the reality of the creatures.

These reports, which are also of the type commonly recorded in the databases of Bigfoot research organizations, are very consistent in descriptive details. Accounts from around the country of the the animal's size and appearance, their tracks, their vocalizations, and their foul stench show very little variation. Observations of the animals' behavior, such as their being heard stalking witnesses, but staying just out of sight, and their apparent marking of territories by twisting and breaking trees and large limbs, show stable patterns. Along with occasional compelling photos and videos, this constitutes a considerable body of physical evidence that there is an undiscovered or unrecognized large, hairy bipedal animal seen, not infrequently, in forested areas in large sections of this country.

Some might think Bigfoot sightings in Southeast Texas, North Carolina, or anywhere in the South, regardless of the details, are the spurious products of wild imaginations or misidentifications of bears or other wildlife heavily influenced by the publicity of the more likely legitimate sightings from the Pacific Northwest. This was the conclusion reached by a panel of experts on *Bigfoot: the Definitive Guide,* a documentary that appeared on cable television in 2011. They rather summarily dismissed sightings in other parts of the country after the Wallace sightings in California in 1958 as being unreliable, attributing the reports as probably coming from people who wanted to be part of the Bigfoot craze. The most these experts would concede about southern sightings is they were almost certainly chance encounters with escapee apes or breeding populations of feral chimpanzees or baboons.

This view is based on the assumption that there was no established history of mystery hominid sightings in the South prior to the famous one in California in 1958. In fact, there was a long tradition of such accounts of unknown ape-like animals in the South, but they tended to be more localized and were known by a variety of different colloquial names like booger, ape-man, and swamp critter. Nobody had put it together, yet that these stories were all about what could only be called mystery hominids or apes. Most people, even if they were aware of their local legends, were unaware that maybe only a couple of counties away there was a virtually identical legend.

In the Big Thicket country, for example, there were published newspaper reports of a naked, hairy wild man seen roaming the woods of Hardin County, Texas, as early as 1952, over six years before the Wallace stories were so heavily popularized. Such stories are duplicated in rural areas throughout the vast region reaching from Texas into Virginia, Kentucky, and the Ohio River basin. However, it wasn't until after the California Bigfoot story came out that many southerners began to realize they were dealing with a similar animal.

The debunking or underestimating of southern Bigfoot traditions also assumes that a large unknown hominid would need millions of acres of forested wilderness like in the Pacific Northwest to survive and to have remained undiscovered by science. It ignores the fact that there are also millions of acres of forested land in the South that could be suitable habitat for highly adaptive primates; and as we will hopefully demonstrate, these beings may be intelligent and crafty enough to live on the margins of human society and remain essentially hidden without the need of vast stretches of land uninhabited by humans.

How and Why We Started Searching for Bigfoot

Tom is a real estate investor and trains lifeguards for a living. He has lived most of his life on property owned by three generations of his family in the North Carolina Blue Ridge country. His land directly adjoins the half-million-acre Pisgah National Forest. At the far end of his property, Tom has a rustic cabin situated a mile and a half off the nearest paved road. It is at the end of an old logging road scraped from the mountainside some forty or fifty years ago and is right up next to a portion of federally protected land set aside as a black bear sanctuary. This is how Tom describes the site where he has had repeated contacts with the unknown creature and how he got into Bigfoot research:

> The property my family owned was two separate
> pieces: one tract of land twenty-six acres complete
> with barn, three creeks and pasture, and the other
> a hundred acres, with some pasture and plenty of
> water. But most of it was virgin land, rough, hilly,

and dense, a perfect habitat for wildlife. A native
trout stream ran right through the middle of our
property and there was nothing above it but mile
after mile of mountains, some almost blue in color
in the distance. The only road through this place was
a small logging road on the side of the mountain. It
was near there that I had my first encounter with a
hairy, ape-like creature in 1991 after being run off a
timber boundary by three of the creatures.

During the fall of that year, I began to hear
something running down the mountain through
the leaves at night, and it always seemed to come
down about the same time every night. At first I
just passed it off as deer coming down to graze in
one of the fields below my house, but as time went
on I noticed the noises were much too heavy for
deer and the movement wasn't uniform like a deer.
After it would come down some nights, I could
hear it return if I was up. When it would come
back, it was slower and I could tell whatever it was,
there was more than one, and it always used my
uncle's logging road or the safety of the creek.

After about a month of this, I decided to take
a closer look. After a night of noises on the road,
the next day I went over to inspect the road in
broad daylight. I walked a little ways and saw
shit everywhere. Whatever it was, it was eating

real good and it had a constant case of diarrhea. I walked a little more and there was still more feces everywhere, a brown-runny kind with corn all in it. Well, it did not take a rocket scientist to figure this out. Whatever it was, it was going into my uncle's cornfield eating hard field corn and then doing a number on his road and my woods. For this kind of a bowel movement it had to be big as hell, or there had to be a whole bunch of them, or both.

After a day or two of thinking about how much feces were on the road, I started to worry a little. I've got something coming through the woods at night, that sounds heavy as hell, it's fast as lightning and it can shit more in one night than I can in a month. Yes, I started paying special attention to this road at night. I wanted to see what this was, and I knew it wasn't bear or deer crap. It just didn't match up.

The next day I went by Duke Power Company and had a telephone pole stuck in the ground and a huge night light attached to the top. It was only eight bucks a month, and I figured it was money well spent. Regardless of the light, the animal still moved at night and I still found crap on my road. One night after a big rain, I went over to the road and followed the feces trail up the mountain through the back part of my place on to the Pisgah

National Forest and finally found a soft spot in the mud. My God, this can't be real, I told myself. I found footprints, kind of bizarre looking, wide at the top, some as wide as fifteen inches and as long as eighteen or twenty inches, tapering off at the base of the heel, making deep impressions in the mud, with what looked like a pad in the middle, and at the end of the toes were claws that extended into the ground below the track. I thought there was no way there could be Bigfoot on my place, but regardless of what I thought, my mind was very quickly changing.

I wanted and needed more information to find out what was really going on. I hadn't really seen anything yet, but I'd sure as hell heard it and had seen where it had been, so I decided to talk to one of the locals who had bear hunted all his life. At first I did not want to come across as some weird-ass who heard burglars in the woods, so I gently made friends with him and watched what he was doing in the woods on my ten acres a little farther up the creek. Besides that, this man had freely used our property for the past twenty years while we were away in Georgia, so I figured he owed me. I could ask him whatever I wanted when the time came.

We continued to be friends. In the past I always noticed he was on our place every day doing

something, but I really didn't know what. Finally I
had won his confidence and we drove in his jeep to
a high ridge on my place. We got out and looked
around. What I saw wasn't a pretty sight—two or
three deer slaughtered, cut up right in the middle,
and hundreds of loaves of bread and sweet cakes
all over the place. I was in shock, there was enough
here for a hundred bears, what to say of just a few.

You could hear the flies blowing the rotting
meat. I almost puked, but held my emotions back.
He started to speak, proud of what he had brought
me to see. This was on my place, and I never knew
anything about it.

"Yep, this is where the bears come to eat. If I didn't
do this, they would starve to death you know."

I stood still in shock. He continued speaking.

"I want you to come hunt with me one night."

"You mean you do it at night when it's illegal as
hell?" I asked.

"Yep, there's nothing like it. You'd love it. We
use dogs and all."

"Have you ever seen anything other than a bear,
anything unusual?" I asked.

"One night we was huntin' close to your place,
behind your house the other side of the mountain,"
he said, "and it took my dogs til four o'clock in
the morning before they treed. When we got there

I shined the light in the tree, a huge sycamore. Whatever it was jumped out—and I've never seen a bear that fuckin' big! It hollered when it hit the ground. Must have jumped out forty feet up, hit the ground a runnin' and run in a straight line. Bears don't do that, they tend to run in circles. Whatever it was, that son of a bitch was as black as tar and it run like it had a fire up its ass."

With what this man had showed me, the tremendous amount of food he was putting out, and his story, I knew I was dealing with a species of animal that hadn't been put on the books yet. To make matters worse, the fucking thing walked by my house nearly every day of my life, and this man was one of the reasons. He didn't know it, but he was feeding the fucking things, too. Out of ignorance he thought he was just feeding the bears, and he'd been doing it for, Christ's sakes, ten or twenty or no telling how many years. The old man was seventy and had been bear hunting on our property all his life.

I put a gate up about a year after this. I wanted the creature to leave, but it never did. The bear hunters continue to use four-wheelers on trails behind my house, and the food was still being put out, just in different places. They wouldn't stop at nothing. The game wardens seemed to promote this type of activity. My hands were tied.

It was thus Tom's life circumstances compelled him into entering the search for answers to the Bigfoot enigma.

Rob is a semi-retired veteran managing editor of Texas weekly newspapers. His first journalism job in 1979 was with the *Kountze News* in the county seat of Hardin County near Sour Lake, the tiny Southeast Texas town where he grew up. Much of the land between those two towns is now included within the Big Thicket National Preserve, administered by the National Park Service. Rob grew up hearing strange stories from an early age about things seen in those woods.

Such tales are a well-established tradition, as people have been seeing weird things in this region for a long time. Before European settlers arrived, the heart of the Big Thicket in Hardin County, which remains the most forested county in Texas, was uninhabited. There is no archeological evidence of permanent Indian settlements in either prehistoric or historic times. They are said to have avoided large sections of those vast, swampy, jungle-like woods due to their supposedly superstitious belief the forest was haunted by demons and evil spirits.

When he was a kid in 1952, the same newspaper he would eventually go to work for in Kountze ran a series of reports of a naked, hairy wild man seen in several places in the nearby woods, including Village Creek where his grandfather frequently took him and his big brother Mickey on fishing and camping trips. Rob's grandpa had also read the newspaper accounts and did not discount them because the sightings were taken seriously enough to result in official investigations by the Hardin County Sheriff Department, which uncovered unexplained large footprints. The rumors made their next trip to Village Creek particularly exciting for Rob and Mickey with the possibility of seeing the unknown beast vivid in their imaginations.

Bigfoot was unheard of back then. The word had not yet even originated out in California, so there was no chance people's imaginations had been influenced by stories coming from the Pacific Northwest. Rational attempts to explain the wild man sightings appealed to theories of an escaped convict or mental patient who had managed to survive in the wild; a crazy old hermit or relict Indian, who delighted in startling astonished witnesses; or maybe a worn-out, mangy old gorilla dumped from the flea-bitten menagerie of some wandering carnival sideshow and left to fend for itself in the near tropical deep woods. It tells you something about the mystique of the Big Thicket that such relatively exotic attempts at explanation would be seriously considered and the sightings would not be summarily dismissed as hoaxers wandering the woods in gorilla suits. Experienced woodsmen and hunters doubted all of these theories.

The wild man was always reported as being barefoot and naked, and as having much more hair than a normal man. Anyone who could survive in those snake- and mosquito-infested woods with no clothes on had their respect, and the fact it did so lent an air of mystery. No normal human being, no matter how crazy, hairy, or desperate, could last long running around naked in those woods. It almost had to be some kind of unknown animal, despite how strange or man-like it might be.

In the next few years there were no sightings reported and the wild man tales coming from the Thicket gradually faded away. By the time Rob graduated from high school and went on to study at the University of Texas in Austin, he quit thinking of the wild man as anything more than superstition and folklore. When he took that job for the Kountze newspaper in 1979, he quickly had his mind changed as he explains:

> I had fond memories of the wild man stories
> reported by the very same newspaper I had gone
> to work for. I assumed they were romantic fairy
> tales of a simpler day and time, but I couldn't help
> but wonder if anything like a wild man had been
> seen in the Hardin County woods since the days
> of my childhood. With this in mind I invited the
> paper's readership to inform me of any unusual
> things they might have seen in the local woods.
> The solicitation was carefully worded and made
> no specific reference to the wild man or any such
> creature so as not to prejudice or affect potential
> responses. The responses I received far exceeded
> my wildest expectations and were stranger than

anything I could ever have imagined. Not only had the wild man been witnessed since the 1950s, it was still being seen up until that time.

A young couple had innocently gone to the local Lover's Lane, where a mysterious spectral "ghost light" was rumored to have been seen many times over the years, naively assuming there was no risk involved. They had not been there long and had just got a glimpse of what they thought might be the light, when something large and hairy pounced on the hood of their pickup and glared at them menacingly. It ran off howling into the woods, leaving claw marks on the pickup's hood, after the gentleman involved in the incident unloaded both barrels of his shotgun at the beast through the windshield.

This was only the most dramatic of the encounters and sightings reported to me at that time. There were others, mostly by people unknown to one another, whose accounts rang true and corroborated one another down to specific details of the wild man's appearance and behavior. That was enough to convince me. I was hooked. I had been transformed from a novice reporter for a backwoods country newspaper to a Bigfoot researcher through no more than having been born where I was, from being in the right place at the right time, and having a naturally healthy journalistic curiosity.

TWO

Tom's Stories from North Carolina

Tom is far from alone in having seen the unknown hairy beasts in western North Carolina. There is a rich tradition of sightings in that region. Here are some of the wonderful tales he has heard since the time he was growing up to the present, as told in Tom's own colorful language. It is Tom speaking in all first-person accounts.

Family Warning

My grandmothers and grandfathers had all advised me not to build my house in the area that I did, but they never told me why. My grandfather planted corn here when I was a child. I would help him plant it. When harvest time would come, something would eat most of it before we ever got it up. I can remember my granddad looking at odd tracks in between the corn rows.

"What kind of tracks are these, Paw Paw?" I asked him.

"Son, if I told you, you wouldn't believe me," he said.

I was only a boy of eight or nine years old, so I just kind of forgot about it, or did not see what was going on. Being the child I was, I didn't really care.

Aunt Kate

When my great, great, Aunt Kate Burnette passed away in 1994, she was a hundred years old and had lived in these mountains all her life. She might have taken the secret of Bigfoot to her grave. She had a few experiences with the monster. Once when she was picking berries they ran her out of the woods. So, evidently these boogers have been here a long time, and still are here.

Old Man Early's Tug-of-War

Old Man Early had about nine hundred acres on the south Catawba River close to Morganton, North Carolina. All he ever did was raise hogs and hunt deer. One afternoon after he had enough of feeding hogs and listening to his Missus nag him, he decided to get in his pickup and go shoot him a buck. He had left plenty of corn out close to the thick rhododendron bushes on the north end of his property and figured it was high time to get that eight-point buck that was pawing up the ground there marking his territory.

He climbed out of his pickup at about 4:30 p.m. around a hundred yards from his deer-baiting area and just settled down behind a blind he had built. Not long after he had got settled in, he heard and saw the biggest buck he had ever laid eyes on. He slowly tightened in his 30–30 Winchester, placed his finger on the trigger, and scoped in for the kill shot. Old Man Early was a crack shot and when he felt for sure, BOOM, the big buck dropped graveyard dead and only kicked a few times before there was no movement at all. Early put his gun in his pickup, put on his gloves, and was ready to drag the deer back to the truck to claim his prize. As he approached the deer he heard a rustling in the bushes behind the big buck. He did not think too much about it and just reached down to get the back legs of the deer and drag. He had only dragged the deer about five feet when he felt the deer pull him back in the opposite direction.

Surely, he thought, something just was not right here. He slowly turned and saw a large black figure and two black, hairy hands pulling on the deer's antlers, dragging in the opposite direction. Early did not want to give up that easy. He tugged again thinking he was dreaming—that this was not real. It was the last thing Early remembered.

He woke up at one o'clock the next morning—naked. All of his clothes had been ripped off except for one sock and one of his boots that were still on. He crawled to his pickup, called for help, and was treated for a mild concussion. Despite bruises and cuts to his body, he was released the next day from Catawba Medical Center in Morganton. Early did not want to talk to authorities about his encounter and only discussed it with a few of his old deer hunting buddies. When he went back to his property, he found where something had dragged the deer high on the mountain ridge, placed the deer off the ground in a huge oak tree, and had eaten both hindquarters off clean to the stump. Old Man Early never set foot in the woods again. Now he just stays at home with his nagging wife, and still raises hogs to this day.

The Ape-man on Buck Creek

Buck Creek runs in another set of mountains between my house, the Blue Ridge Parkway and Curtis Creek. I had just finished writing an article for the newspaper about Bigfoot in the area, and an old woman called the newspaper to warn me about the "nastiness" out there. I never got to talk to the woman but recalled the story from the receptionist at the local paper the next day. She somehow had lost my number to give to the old woman and the woman never got mine, but this is how the story goes.

She said her friend had just got back from World War II as a highly decorated veteran and had a reputation as a great hunter in and around McDowell County. He had heard the story of a monstrous-type ape that lived behind a waterfall up Buck Creek. Buck Creek starts at the Parkway and winds its way down into Lake Tahoma, where all the rich people live. It kind of follows Highway 80, crosses Highway 70 at the bottom of the mountain, and eventually empties into the Catawba River basin. Needless to say, it is rough, wild land the same as the area where I live.

Anyhow, the man's name was also Buck, and hell, Buck had been killing Germans and Italians and Japanese people for four and a half years, so he decided he was going to go in and kill this demon that people said lived behind the falls at Buck Creek. It had been rumored the monster was running hunters out of the area for some time now, and Buck's ego, unfortunately, was bigger than his ass. This woman did not want me to suffer the same fate as Buck, so this was her way of trying to help me.

She said Buck went into the area and did not come out. They sent in a hunting party the next day and found Buck's gun had fired off several rounds, but there was no blood from the monster. Only Buck's head was found on the ground, and they never retrieved his body. Apparently the monster had bitten his head off or ripped it off. Anyway, it did not sound good to me.

After I heard the story, it sent shivers up and down my spine, but I thought, what is going to kill me when sometimes I bring it food? It, or they, have munched on a few of my dogs, but maybe I still won't get eaten or killed. Sometimes when you're so far in, there just isn't a way out. I could leave and sell my property and go to Florida, but I just am not quite ready yet.

Uncle Lee Burnette and the Moonshine Varmint

My uncle Lee Burnette was an old farmer, a whale of a man, simple and hard-working, who stood about six-foot-two and never wore anything during the week but a pair of overalls and a pair of army boots. Him and my grandparents were the only people I ever knew of that managed to get kicked out of the Baptist church for square dancing on Saturday night only to work their way back into the church later on and become Sunday school teachers. Back in the first part of the last century, church rules were, to say the least, a bit strict. During the week, Uncle Lee made liquor up on the mountain for a little extra money to accompany his cattle business. He had just moved his new still high on the mountain where he could clearly see the valley below so he could run if need be to elude the local revenue agents. Anxious to see how his new still was working, he had left a flunky helping him make liquor, and it was time for a shift relief. It was Uncle Lee's time at the helm of the still, so he hurried up the mountain at daylight.

They quickly exchanged shifts and Uncle Lee was ready to take a sample of the cooking corn squeezings from the night before. After about three swigs of the moonshine brandy, his body began to feel real good and the daylight was peeping over the horizon. Imagine this: the cooking whiskey smelled real good to a drunk, but if you did not drink, the air was rather putrid, a bitter stinking smell.

Lee took another drink and heard a crashing sound on top of the mountain. Bam! Bop! Bam! came down the mountain. Lee described the monster as a large ape-man weighing at least five hundred pounds that could leap twenty to thirty feet in a single bound. The ape came down the hill Rambo-style until it looked directly into my uncle's eyes. He thought he was looking at the devil, but quickly realized the devil couldn't have stunk that bad. The creature looked at the still, looked at my uncle, sniffed the air, and quickly vanished over the side of the mountain. The incident did not deter my uncle from making liquor, and he continued doing so in the mountains. But from then on he was wielding a double-barreled shotgun. Who knows, but he used to say that varmint might've been after his liquor. He told his story in the valley and the locals made fun of him. They knew his reputation for making bootleg whiskey and told Lee the ape-man or Bigfoot came out of his bottle of moonshine. Uncle Lee shared his story with me, but after that he quit telling it outside the family.

Honeymoon for Neighbors

My sister told me an interesting story about a young couple who moved about two miles from here on a mountain on the other side of Highway 70. It was their honeymoon evening. The week before, they had a small bulldozer push in a road and flatten out a place for a double-wide. Everything was so romantic. All of their dreams were coming true. They had bought an acre at a rock-bottom price, had a new home, and to top if off, a new life with each other.

When they arrived, Jimmy didn't pay much attention to the old woman who lived nearby on the mountain when she told him there were all kinds of varmints in those woods. He just kind of laughed—after all, he'd only asked her about the deer hunting on the mountain—although it did seem to him her answer was a little weird.

That evening was so perfect for the two of them. They had just gotten married, there was a small fire burning in the fireplace, they had a bottle of chilled champagne, and Jimmy had just finished making love to his new bride. All they could hear were a few crickets singing out a new melody to them. They were in love with their new home and with each other.

Then terror came seemingly from nowhere, like an evil dance by a witch doctor. Melanie looked at Jimmy.

"Jimmy, there's something scratching on our bedroom wall. Honey, do you hear it?"

"Yeah, I hear it, but what in God's name is it? We've got no flashlight and no outdoor lights, and I ain't going out there by myself to see what it is."

The scratching got louder and more distinct like it was made by something hard and rigid. Suddenly it seemed like it was coming from up and down the whole length of their new home. Then it stopped abruptly and lapsed into silence for about two minutes.

"It's all right," Jimmy said. "It's probably just a dog."

Melanie was relieved and kissed Jimmy on the cheek. "I love you," she said.

The terror from hell came back with a vengeance, this time pushing on the walls. The entire house moved. They watched in horror as the walls slowly buckled and cracked. Something was pushing on the walls. The sheetrock by the edge of the bed split. The whole bedroom window and frame came crashing down next at the foot of their bed, pushed in from the outside. Jimmy ran down the hall just as a pair of hairy, ape-like hands withdrew from the gaping hole where the window had been a moment before.

"In the name of God, help me!" he yelled.

After thirty minutes of prayer crouched in the bathtub, they mustered the courage to leave and rent a motel room. They never lived there after that, and only went back to get their things and to have their mobile home moved.

The Fishermen

Two fishermen saw two apes above the water intake above the watershed yesterday. They said the apes were brown and were walking on two legs bent over with arms dragging the ground. One of the guys is a registered taxidermist.

The Big Monkey

A person visited me who claims he played with a large monkey when he was a small boy. He seemed credible, considering his family had been exposed to somewhat familiar circumstances concerning a few Bigfoot. Most of their activity was back in the early seventies. Their home also borders Pisgah National Forest, but they're about nine miles away, which leads me to think southern Appalachia might have as many as a few hundred of these so-called monsters.

He claimed to have been playing in the woods near his home, when out of the woods came a small child-like ape. He said they played in the forest, went up on the hillside, and met another ape-like creature, which acted like it was not at all thrilled by his presence and seemed to scold the young one for bringing him along. They then brought him back to his yard and simply left.

The most interesting thing about his encounter was that when the animals walked their arms were so long that their knuckles would scrape the ground. He also said they were of fairly small stature, which could mean they were very young and not yet fully grown.

Tim and Robbey's Visit

One time I had two friends come over after work. They arrived before I did. They didn't have the keys to my place, so they thought they would enjoy the cool of the evening having some beer on my front porch. They sat with no electricity enjoying the sound of the creek running. They downed a couple of cool ones, when they heard heavy footsteps on the logging road.

Tim and Robbey saw a pair of red eyes looking at them. The monster then beat its chest and ran, tearing up the forest as it went.

I asked Robbey about it and he said, "Whatever it was, it's one big mean fucker with an attitude problem. The next time I sit on your porch, Tom, it will be with a light and a gun. That thing scared the shit out of me."

My friend no longer drinks and is now a traveling preacher. He told me he thought it was the devil after him. I don't particularly believe that, but the beast has certainly got my attention more than once. Yes, it's made a believer out of me, but I don't believe the "Booger Man" runs wild in the woods scaring people out of sin into a new existence. It just happened to work that way for my friend. To me, to not even have a beer is downright un-American.

THREE

Rob's Stories from the Big Thicket

Like the area around Pisgah National Forest in North Carolina, there is a long history of big, hairy mystery creature sightings in rural Southeast Texas. Here are examples as told by Rob. Preference is given to his own experiences and direct eyewitness accounts, but the first case is a previously secret story from a respectable Sour Lake family Rob knows well.

They Don't Eat Horses, Do They?

After the publication of my first book, several people from Sour Lake and from other small towns and rural communities in the Big Thicket region came forth to tell me stories of their own or family members' encounters with ape-like monsters. The first one was from Mrs. Ann Bazan, the mother of my high school classmate and close friend, Dennis. The witness was her father, Mr. Pitre. Fearing ridicule, the story was never told to anyone outside the family before. Mrs. Bazan was willing to tell me about the incident because she had known me since I was a little kid and was glad someone was finally taking such stories seriously.

Back in the early 1920s when they first laid the oil pipelines through Texas, Mr. Pitre had a job horseback riding along the right-of-way cleared from the woods to check the pipeline for leaks. At the time, this was the best way to do the job, and he was the first to do it in these parts. One time he was a few miles west of the Kountze-Sour Lake highway not far from where the pipeline crosses Little Pine Island Bayou, when his horse started to act funny.

It was getting fidgety, wide-eyed and nervous, like it was sensing some nearby danger, and it started to buck. Pitre was about to lose control of the horse, so he dismounted and tried to calm it down. The horse bolted away from him and headed off down the pipeline. It only got about twenty yards when something came out of the woods and grabbed it.

The thing looked like a huge, hairy man over seven feet tall. It was naked and completely covered with long, shaggy hair like an ape and had a barrel chest. While Pitre watched in terror, the monster wrapped its enormous arms around the horse, twisted its head, and broke its neck. Mrs. Bazan said her father was never able to forget the terrified whinnies and cries from that horse.

Naturally, he feared for his own life, but after the horse was dead the thing didn't threaten him. It just turned and stared at Pitre before it dragged the horse into the woods. This gave him a chance to get a good look at it. There was no mistaking what he in horror had seen with his own two eyes.

The Face in the Window

After my first appearance on Art Bell's show, I received over four hundred e-mails from around the country. The personally most compelling of these seemed to confirm my contention that the Big Thicket Wild Man in Southeast Texas, the Fouke Monster in the Arkansas Delta, the Honey Island Swamp Monster near New Orleans, and the Rougarou of the South Louisiana Bayou Country are all more than mere legends. One such message came from a kid named Chris Adams who lived just outside Liberty, Texas near the Trinity River swamps, which are generally considered the western edge of the Big Thicket and are also the southern and western limit of the great southern cypress swamps that extend all the way from there to Virginia.

In the mid-1990s when he was in middle school, Chris and his family lived in a mobile home on land they owned out in the Trinity swamps. His parents were usually up and off to work before dawn, and Chris would have about an hour to get up after they left and get ready to go to school. One morning after his parents had left, and about five minutes after he woke up, he heard a loud bang on the side of the trailer toward the front. He could not imagine what could have delivered such a blow, which literally shook the entire house. He got up to investigate and walked toward the front of the trailer from his bedroom in back.

As he passed a window in the kitchen, he could hear the creature making a commotion outside in the dark. Slowly he pulled back the mini blinds and found himself staring face to face with what he described as a hairy, man-shaped being with huge, glowing yellow eyes. Stunned with terror, he dropped to the floor and crawled back to his bedroom where he grabbed his shotgun and lay in his bed clenching it, fearful the creature might try to break into the trailer and doubtful whether his gun was of a big enough gauge to stop it.

When daylight finally came, he cautiously went outside, still clenching his shotgun, and found evidence something had been there. There were no prints, but the ground was disturbed. Judging from the height of the kitchen window and the fact the trailer was set about two and a half feet off the ground Chris estimated the thing he saw had to be close to seven feet tall.

These stories verified that the wild man was seen in the Big Thicket long before the 1950s reports in the Kountze newspaper were published. The tales coming from the nearby woods also confirmed my suspicion that such creatures have long had a widespread presence in East Texas.

The Arkansas Hog Killer

A vivid eyewitness report I received from Arkansas confirmed my further suspicion similar Bigfoot-type animals would likely be seen in the extensive swamps and woodlands of the adjoining southern states. The following is an excerpt from Randell Homsley's e-mail:

> I caught your show with Barbara Simpson on
> *Coast to Coast*, and although neither I nor any
> of my family have ever talked about some of the
> things we have experienced, I thought I would
> drop you a line. First, let me say that I am a former
> Marine and I have been a law-enforcement officer
> here in Arkansas for over ten years. I am not prone
> to relating stories that I don't have all the facts
> about. My family and I had a deer camp just west
> of Gurdon, Arkansas, for about fifteen years.
>
> What I want to relate to you concerns sightings
> by my family members of Bigfoot in our hunting
> area. I have never personally seen the creature
> called Bigfoot, but I do believe I have seen its
> offspring. My father-in-law and uncle have seen
> him, and my father-in-law as a matter of fact
> refuses to go into those woods at night anymore.

I have nevertheless sensed and smelled what I believe to be the creature called Bigfoot.

While on my way to my stand early one morning, I heard a wild commotion in the woods ahead of me. I heard a wild hog squealing and then after a moment, it was silent. After I took a moment to check my drawers I took a few steps forward and heard something bounding away. I raised my flashlight up the trail and just going off to the right side of the trail I saw what looked like a two- or three-foot-tall monkey, that's the only way I know to describe it. It was too slender to be a baby bear, and it was walking on its hind legs.

Anyway, I waited about twenty minutes for daylight, and then just off the path about ten yards out in the woods to my right, I saw a wild hog with its throat and part of its belly ripped open lodged in a tree about eight feet off the ground.

It's easy to see from this why Randell thought he saw the baby Bigfoot, and why he deduced it was the momma or poppa who stuck the hog up in the tree. Significantly, this sighting not only provides evidence to the widespread occurrence of ape-like creatures in the Deep South, but it also gives a clue to Bigfoot's hunting and dietary habits.

The Tyler County Squirrel Hunter's Story

One of the most memorable hunter sightings related to me came from a gentleman (who asked to not be named) I met at a conference in Jefferson, Texas, in 2001 sponsored by the Texas Bigfoot Research Center.

"What brings you to the conference?" I asked when he approached the table where I had set up to sell my book. "Are you a member of the Texas Bigfoot Research group?"

"Nope," he responded simply.

His expression told me he wasn't sure he wanted to talk to me, but he appeared desperate to talk to somebody.

"I saw me one of them damn things," he hesitantly confided, still looking me up and down as if trying to judge whether I would believe him, or if he should even bother telling me about his experience. "I didn't know we were supposed to have critters such as that in East Texas, and I wanted to find out what other folks had to say about them."

"Do you mind telling me the details of your sighting?" I asked, trying to draw him out and make him more comfortable with me. "How close were you to it?"

"Just as close as I am to you right now," he said from across the table. "I damn near stepped on the son of a bitch. I was out squirrel hunting over in Tyler County in the Thicket. I spotted a big ol' fox squirrel up in a tall pin oak tree and was sneaking up on it looking up into the tree while raising my shotgun and trying to draw a bead on that squirrel's bushy behind. That damn Bigfoot was sitting on the ground fast asleep leaning up against the base of that oak tree. When I fired at that squirrel, it woke him up."

I had never talked to anyone who had had such a close up encounter before and was a little taken aback.

"What did you do?" I finally managed to ask him.

"You see that man over there wearing that white T-shirt?" he asked.

"Yep," I responded.

"I turned just as white as that T-shirt!" he admitted.

"You had a shotgun," I said. "If it was threatening you, why didn't you just shoot it in self-defense?"

He looked at me, with pity on his face, as if I was obviously the stupidest thing on the face of the earth for suggesting such a course of action.

"Are you kidding me? If I would've shot that damned thing with squirrel shot, as big as it was, it wouldn't have done nothing but piss it off. The only thing I could do was turn tail and run."

If there had been a lie detector present, I would have bet anyone a week's pay that fellow's story would have passed with flying colors. There was no doubt in my mind. I talked to several other people at that conference and have since been contacted by a number of people who have had similar sighting experiences. Some of them were almost as dramatic as this squirrel hunter's was, and most of these came from other hunters.

Chester Moore and Radio Call-Ins

Several eyewitness reports from hunters in the Big Thicket, including one who was to become a valuable research ally, have come to me from call-ins to radio programs. In early 2002, not long after the conference in Jefferson, Texas, I appeared on KLVI Radio in Beaumont. My host, Don Briscoe, suspected there would be considerable interest among his listeners in my treatment of the ghost light on Bragg Road in my first book. Don had been in Southeast Texas long enough to have heard at least parts of the legend. He had little doubt there would be callers who wanted to talk about their sightings of the light, real or imagined.

Don had already read the book and was impressed by the evidence I presented to show the Bragg Road light was similar to many that appear regularly around America and throughout the world. I had pretty much convinced him it is a genuine mystery and is associated with energy of an unknown origin. He also knew the Ghost Road, as Bragg Road has come to be known, has been a popular destination for decades for those seeking an encounter with the unknown.

What Don didn't buy into was the idea I developed in the book that the ghost light, or the energy which produces it, has anything to do with unknown hairy hominids. He respectfully questioned whether witness claims of sightings of Bigfoot-type creatures in the vicinity of, and actually on the Ghost Road itself, weren't the product of overactive imaginations.

Don quite frankly did not believe we would get any calls from listeners who had seen such hairy beasts in the nearby forests, so he arranged for Chester Moore to call in. Chester had a weekly outdoors sports show that was featured on the same radio station. Don was vaguely aware that Chester, who was also a hunting guide and animal tracks expert, had claimed on his show there could be some kind of unknown ape in the Big Thicket.

A few minutes before we were to go on the air, Don asked me to test the volume on the headphone set I would be using. Curiously, just as I put them on, the control board in the studio blacked out. Don and the show's producer frantically and unsuccessfully tried to find out what had gone wrong, when just seconds before air time, the control board came back on as mysteriously as it had blacked out.

"Those damned lights must be following me around, Don," I joked. "You know, this is exactly what the lights do on Bragg Road. They temporarily knock out electrical systems. So do the hairy wild man creatures. That's one reason I think they are somehow related."

Don grinned, but had little time to digest this information or to analyze what must be a perfectly logical reason for the board to have malfunctioned in the few seconds remaining before we went on the air.

Within a very short while, we began receiving calls from listeners who had actually been to the Ghost Road and seen the infamous light. Not surprisingly, much of the information we got was typical of what I had recorded in my book. People had seen the light up close. There was no doubt in their minds what they had seen.

Much to Don's surprise, when we opened the discussion up to ape-like creature sightings, we immediately received two calls before Chester could get through. One was from a lady who claimed to have seen a pair of huge, two-legged, hairy creatures near a swimming hole on a bayou near Port Arthur some thirty years earlier, before the area was urbanized and was still heavily wooded. One of them was much larger than the other, suggesting an adult and juvenile pair, precisely what would be expected of a real breeding animal.

A man from Vidor claimed he saw a tall ape-looking something crossing a power line right-of-way cut through deep woods near a bayou in Orange County.

Don was clearly amazed by these two accounts and perhaps even more amazed at my confidence in assuring him beforehand we would get such calls. But he had already arranged to have Chester call in, and as it turned out, I was glad he did.

"Ladies and gentlemen," Don announced, "I have asked our next caller, Chester Moore, to join the conversation. Chester has a weekly outdoors show here on KLVI and is a widely respected outdoors journalist and wildlife expert. Chester, in your experience as a professional hunting guide and from your knowledge of animal tracks, have you ever found any tracks in the Big Thicket area that you could not identify?"

"Yes sir, I have," Chester responded without hesitation.

He went on to describe tracks he had seen and recorded with castings from Newton and Orange counties in Southeast Texas that were not those of any animal known to be native to the region.

"In my opinion these tracks are from some undiscovered ape or large primate animal."

I was impressed by Chester's forthrightness. He was willing to risk his credibility as a wildlife expert, on which he depends for making a living. His attitude was the facts speak for themselves. He could show you the tracks and you could make up your own mind, but he was going to stick by his own expert opinion. Something was making these tracks, and whatever it was, it was not a human being or any known animal.

For years I had known of no one else, except for some fast-vanishing old-timers and a handful of actual eyewitnesses, who would even seriously entertain the possibility of there being anything remotely like a Bigfoot in the East Texas woods. I was pretty much out on a limb by myself in publicly claiming through the media that the creatures were there. When I learned about Chester's work, I was thrilled an authoritative contemporary researcher could corroborate their existence.

Chester had done his research, and he made a good case for Bigfoot's existence throughout the Piney Woods ecosystem in East Texas, Arkansas, Louisiana, and southeastern Oklahoma.

"There's good habitat for these creatures all the way from Orange up to Toledo Bend Reservoir on the Sabine. That's over a hundred miles by the river, and the swamp's about ten miles wide taking both sides of the river into account. That adds up to over a thousand square miles of prime habitat. There are only three roads that cross the river between here and Toledo Bend and only a few small towns along that stretch of the river. I'd say there's plenty of room for them to hunt and forage while staying hidden. There's never anybody out here to bother them except a few fishermen and hunters, and even then it's pretty easy for them to stay out of view with all the cover these woods provide."

Chester went on to point out Toledo Bend Reservoir extends up almost another hundred miles on the Texas/Louisiana border and there had been a history of sightings on both sides of the lake. From there going north the watery, leafy wilderness extends up through Caddo Lake, which historically is also the scene of sightings.

From Caddo Lake the network of woods, swamps, creeks, and bottomlands extends on up to the Sulphur River bottoms in Northeast Texas and southern Arkansas near the Louisiana border where there is also evidence of prolonged Bigfoot activity. This is the scene of *The Legend of Boggy*

Creek, the movie based on multiple Bigfoot sightings near Fouke, Arkansas, over forty years ago.

This would only account for the Sabine and Sulphur river systems. About thirty miles to the west of the Sabine is the Neches River, and another thirty miles west of the Neches is the Trinity River. Both of these systems have extensive riverine swamps, and I have received numerous reports of sightings in both areas. And, of course, the Big Thicket with its long history of wild man sightings lies between the Trinity and the Neches.

East of the Sabine in Louisiana is the vast Atchafalaya Basin swamp near Lafayette, where the Cajuns have legends of a Bigfoot-type creature they call the Rougarou, slang for *loup garoux* or werewolf. Near New Orleans, the Honey Island Swamp has long been the scene of hairy monster sightings.

"All told there are tens of thousands of square miles in East Texas, Louisiana, Arkansas, and Southeastern Oklahoma alone, including several national forests, which are equal in remoteness and inaccessibility to the mountain ranges of the Pacific Northwest," Chester said. "It is entirely feasible there could be an unknown animal that escapes our detection in such a vast area. And this does not even include legends of similar animals from Florida, Georgia, Alabama, Tennessee, and the Carolinas which date back to Cherokee times."

Chester made it clear he thought Bigfoot was only a species of undiscovered ape. Unlike me, he did not think there was any connection to weird energies or light-forms or that the animals had any kind of unusual or special abilities beyond what would be expected of a normal animal. Despite our disagreements, I was encouraged a man of his expertise, integrity, and objectivity could at least confirm the beasts—whatever their nature might be—were out there.

Ringing the Bell

A short time after the Beaumont interview, I had the opportunity to appear on the *Coast to Coast* show back when Art Bell was still the host. They had so many hits during the interview that their website crashed. The next morning there were close to four hundred combined e-mails and postings on my website guest book. Most of them were from southerners who were unable to get through by phone to tell their stories. Two calls that did get through were highly significant.

During the interview, I told the story of a likely wild man encounter I experienced one night on a pipeline right-of-way near Little Pine Island Bayou between Sour Lake and Beaumont when I heard a loud animal vocalization. A man called and said he knew exactly where I was talking about. He had been hunting deer there for years on land owned by a hunting club he belonged to. A couple of times he also had heard something howling in the woods at night he thought had to be from some kind of animal not known to inhabit those woods.

Art had no sooner confirmed that the caller did not know me and had never heard of me than another call came in.

"Art, I can back up both of those stories," he said. "My company has a hunting lease in the same area Rob and that other guy talked about on what sounds like it might be the same pipeline. One morning just after sunrise, I saw something big and tall walk across the right-of-way maybe a hundred yards away. There was no doubt it was not human. It had no clothes on and was completely covered with hair. I was so surprised and shocked I did not go to investigate. Even if I could have caught up with it in the thick woods, I wasn't going to risk it. That thing was huge, and I had no idea what it might be capable of doing."

I had noticed a couple of hunting camps consisting of used RVs, old mobile homes, and ramshackle portable buildings in the woods just off the pipeline, but had not mentioned them to Art, so the callers' stories checked out. We also confirmed that the callers were unknown both to me and one another.

"I can believe you guys could possibly have experienced the same thing in the same place," Art commented, "if for no other reason than you all sound alike, with the same distinct Texas accent."

Reports from the Authorities

It may be asked if Bigfoot are so widely seen in East Texas, why they have not been reported by the authorities of state or federally managed forests? The answer is the same as why many witnesses never reported their sightings to the authorities or spoke about them to anyone outside their families. It is the simple fear of not being believed and the possible repercussions on one's career. Here are a couple of examples:

One November afternoon a few years ago on the first day of deer hunting season, as I was returning to my car after taking photos in the Lance Rosier Unit of the Big Thicket National Preserve, I was hailed by a State of Texas Game Warden. After showing him I was unarmed and had no need of a hunting license, I showed him my camera and explained to him I was looking for pictures to illustrate a book I was working on. When I mentioned my name, to my surprise, he said he had read my first book with considerable interest.

After getting my assurance I would not quote him by name, he acknowledged he had received and investigated several reports, both from the Thicket and from Sam Houston National Forest, of Bigfoot encounters. In one incident a witness saw a huge, hairy, upright creature carrying a two-hundred-pound grown hog under its arm like it was a sack of potatoes.

Another case he personally investigated involved some kind of animal picking up a similar-sized hog, gutting it, and lifting it over a six-foot-high wire-link fence with the gate locked. He saw the tracks and the bloody trail the thing left heading off into the swamp and concluded whatever did this was not any animal known to exist in East Texas.

"It wouldn't surprise me if some kind of unknown ape was in these woods. I know from experience there are backwater sloughs and swamps on both the Trinity River and the Neches River which are so inaccessible nobody ever goes there—not even hunters. There are lots of places where these things could hole up and nobody would ever see them or suspect they were there," the Game Warden told me.

Even though he still held out the possibility the apelike creatures were likely to be a small breeding population of an escaped exotic species, he ended our conversation by offering another highly intriguing observation.

"While I was in training for this job, I took a course on native Texas wildlife. The instructor got to the list of large mammals. When he got through, I asked him, what about the black panther? He told me there was no such thing as a large black wild cat anywhere in Texas, and that was just folklore.

"Mister," he went on, "I didn't press the matter, but I saw a black panther with my own eyes on a hunting trip in East Texas only a few years ago. I was standing no more than fifteen or twenty feet from it. It was the most magnificent animal I have ever seen. If the experts can be wrong about the black panthers, they can be wrong about Bigfoot, too, I guess."

Note that the Game Warden's stories and observations corroborate Randell's in terms of the southern Bigfoot apparently having an appetite for wild hogs.

At the time of this writing an additional possible validation of the existence of the mysterious ape creatures came to us from yet another official source. A ranger from the education outreach program of the Big Thicket National Preserve, who asked not to be named, told me one of the other rangers heard an indescribably loud howl while kayaking on the Pine Island Bayou.

"It was as loud as a locomotive," she told me, "and my colleague could not conceive of any animal known to live in the Preserve able to produce such a sound."

The sound had a quality to it similar to the howl of a howler monkey, only it was deeper-pitched and more prolonged—like it could have come from a larger primate. I knew the sound the ranger was talking about. I had heard it myself more than ten years before and no more than a few miles from where the kayaking ranger heard it. It was that experience, which is detailed in the upcoming section about my investigations, that convinced me beyond any doubt Bigfoot live in the Big Thicket.

FOUR

Tom's Investigations

This section comes from Tom's personal experiences and encounters as detailed in his unpublished field notes recorded from 1999, when his first book was released, up to the present. All of these encounters occurred on Tom's land bordering the national forest. They further illustrate what originally got him involved in Bigfoot investigative work and how he began to develop essential elements of the research strategy of attempting to attract the creatures that this book sets forth. It is Tom speaking in all first-person accounts.

First Encounters

The first time I saw the Bigfoot creature face to face, he came within about eight feet from me. It was about four in the afternoon. I had been walking my property line next to the half million-acre Pisgah National Forest where my property stops against the upper edge of Mackey Mountain. My uncle's property joins mine as well there. Our property boundary was a large pile of rocks. The terrain is very rough and very few men have ever been through this area. Besides that, if someone were hunting there, he could never get his game out because there are no roads.

That particular day I had piled up a lot of rocks, three piles to be exact. I had been making a lot of noise moving those rocks. I sat down to rest for about five minutes and got a drink of water out of the stream when I heard something running off the top of the mountain. It sounded like there were two or three different movements in the woods moving very fast, like a cat running. I continued to squat, just knowing I was going to see a big bear or a herd of deer coming right at me. I looked up and saw nothing, but I did hear something running right up to where I was. The only thing between me and it was a large red oak, which was only eight to ten feet away, where the running had stopped.

The next thing I thought was that this wasn't a bear or a deer, because there is no way any wildlife could come that close to a human and hide only a few feet away. I clasped the small 25-caliber pistol in my back pocket, not even bothering to take it out. I knew it wasn't strong enough to kill anything, and besides that, this little gun would only make something wild real mad. That would be a good way for me to get hurt, I thought.

The next thing I knew, I was being pelted with small rocks and stones. I was starting to get very afraid, so I started to talk to whatever it was behind the tree. The more I talked, the worse the stone throwing became. I stood up, took one step, and turned to look back at my attacker. What I saw was a very large black head with eyes that looked amazed at me. It looked at me for about forty-five seconds—no eyeblink, no movement, just a look of astonishment. The face looked half human, half ape, and it occurred to me that it was about fifteen years old. The next thing I remember was thinking I needed to do something.

So, I said to the Bigfoot, "Okay, I'll leave now."

I started to walk back home. Mind you, I did not run, either. I walked slowly, trying to figure out what to do next. I had now seen Bigfoot, the murderer of my dogs, which had disappeared one at a time in the last few months only to have me to find them a few days after going missing with their bones picked clean of flesh. I didn't want him to eat me or take me off somewhere in the mountains where no one could find me. Believe me, I knew this was going to be the hardest thing I'd ever gone through in my life, but I was going to tackle it head on. I was going to get through this and hopefully make a friend out of the giants.

The following week, all I could think of was the face I saw in the woods. I told my mother about it, but it's hard to explain to anyone that you've come face to face with a monster from a different world. I knew I shouldn't shoot it or kill it, but I wanted to be safe. I bought a gun book to study up on what type of rifle I would need to kill this thing, if for some reason I had to. There was always the possibility it could come into my home one night, and I sure as hell needed some kind of a card to play if it did. I refused to be left defenseless, so I decided on a gun big enough to do the job, if it ever came to that.

I purchased an Australian hunting rifle, 303-caliber, with an accurate kill range of four hundred yards. This type of gun had been successfully used during the Boer War in South Africa during the first part of the 1900s and later adapted for government use during World War II. It was called an assassin's rifle because of its deadly accuracy and tremendous knockdown power. I felt a little better about my nights alone at home, but even with this gun, I was still very respectfully afraid of these unknown creatures.

I had no real intentions of shooting any of these beasts, and would only do so as a last resort. They sure as hell weren't afraid of me or they wouldn't have come out of hiding. They had stayed out of sight for centuries, with a sighting being reported only ever now and then, and nobody ever really knowing what it was they saw. These creatures evidently felt sort of at ease with me for some unknown reason—why else would they put themselves on display for me to gander at?

I refused to change my whole life because of the ape-men living on my property, and I really just couldn't abandon my home. One night, not long after my first sighting and after I had seen the creatures several more times from a distance on my property, I could hear them very cautiously approaching the edge of my yard. I could also smell their stench. I couldn't handle seeing them in broad daylight, much less in the dark of night. I had been in the backyard alone playing my music loud and standing around a fire I had built. They must've been attracted to the activity. I put out the fire with the water hose and cut off the music and walked to the center of my house in the hallway, trying to think what I should do next. The odor was getting horrible; it seemed to penetrate the walls like a sharp knife. My dog was beginning to whine behind me. The stench got worse, almost like sulfur burning.

I looked down the hallway out the window of my back bedroom. Outside was a head gaping at me with red glowing eyes. Its head filled my whole window. When it saw me look at it, it turned its head briefly and moved away from my line of sight. My dog continued to whine. I said to myself, I am getting the hell out of here tonight. I jumped from the porch into my car, leaving my poor dog to fend for himself. I spent the night at my mother's.

The next day I noticed muddy handprints, with short, stubby fingers, large palms, and a huge thumb (almost seven inches long) on the outside walls all the way around my house. There was one print near the window where it had gaped at me, one by the air conditioner, and another on my front porch between the sliding glass doors. I believe maybe they were trying to kidnap me. I had read where occasionally they would pick up loners and take them far into the mountains where the victim couldn't find his way home. God, I prayed this wouldn't be my destiny. As big as they were, I wouldn't be able to stop them.

I examined the window where it had looked in at me. From the ground to the base of the window, it's seven and a half feet, so this thing had to be eight feet tall at a minimum. Either that or he had one of his buddies on his back, but that's fairly doubtful. I took pictures of the print, examined footprints in the yard and wished so desperately for someone to help me with this thing. I was hopelessly alone, and it seemed every time I told a friend what was going on in my life, they either weren't interested or really just didn't give a shit. I was going to get through this, and I had made up my mind not to give up my home because of them.

They could get me in the meantime, but that was the chance I was going to take. Besides that I couldn't afford to build another house. I had all my money sunk into this one. I was stuck between a rock and a hard place, but I refused to let Bigfoot get me down completely. I needed to try to make friends of them somehow. They were going to be there anyway, so I decided to make the best of it.

Feeding the Creatures

My whole outlook began to change. With my determination to make friends with it, I was also trying to bury my fears. This was truly the hardest thing I had faced in my life, and it was going to determine much of how I would handle the rest of my life. I started going by grocery stores and begging for produce so I could feed this thing. I was going to be its pal. Sometimes I would get fruit, bread and bakery items, apples, grapes, bananas, lettuce, or anything they were fixing to throw out. I set up a system where I would put food out on the mountain, pick up a rock or laurel limb and beat three times on a tree, signaling them where the food was. Soon I had a response.

Within weeks, it was working. They would come and even mimic my knock three times. I was amazed and still a little scared, but I tried to take food as often as I could. My system was working, but I was still carrying some mixed emotions. I might make the damn things tame, and then what would I do?

Sometimes when I would go to feed them, they would sound like they were trying to tear a whole tree down. I guess that was to scare off others from the food. What I didn't realize was that the sugar in the cakes was making for some bad dispositions, but I had to take whatever food the bakeries would give me at good prices. So, again, I had another problem.

In the evenings after dark, they would stand on my uncle's property behind a wood pile and watch my house. Their eyes had a distinct red glow, almost orange-colored. It was scary, but I could not let this thing go, at least not for now anyway. I was totally mesmerized by them. One variable I hadn't considered was their response. I did not know what to do, but I had not thought that maybe they didn't know what to do either. Their reaction to me was probably just as mixed as mine was to them.

I did not become a Bigfoot researcher and writer by choice. It was only because there was so much going on around me that it would be a shame to waste the strangeness of it all. Are all the people all over the world who have seen mysterious hairy primates experiencing a mass illusion? I think not.

The Danger of Dependence

I do not want these creatures becoming dependent on me for food or survival. I will start to wean and limit the amount of food that I take to the forest for feeding. The initial reason at the onset for the food was the simple purpose of making friends. But at this point, it is getting out of hand because they are always around wanting a handout. It will be necessary to continue to put out food to satisfy my curiosity and in order to get an adequate photograph of them, but I do not want to completely throw these beasts off from their normal mode of foraging in the forest for food.

For a while there, I was feeding them so regularly that even when my sister and mother would visit my home and walk behind my house, they, too, were getting a response from the Bigfoot. They told me about hearing the banging on the trees. I feared that maybe I was domesticating them too fast. This was not what I wanted at all. I wanted proof that they exist. Then I could help them, but domestication of a wild human or ape—forget it! He's better off eating roots and frogs.

Studies show that genetically we are less than one percent different from an ape or chimpanzee. I was also afraid that too close contact with humans might wipe them out. Remember what the Spaniards did to the Aztecs? Remember what we did to the poor American Indians with the diseases we gave them? More were killed from transmittable diseases than with the rifle. Their blood paved streets and painted our homes. We need to be ashamed of what we did to the Indians.

For a long time now, I have been trying to get a photo close-up way up on the creek near my cabin trailer. It's important for the reader here to understand why I am trying to get photos at that place instead of the ease and comfort of simply walking behind my house and easily setting up my equipment there. Although I am aware of more activity here at home, for the past year I have tried somewhat successfully to control their activity to a minimum. After all, I've got to live here and feeding here on a regular basis tends to make them here all the time. I've proved several times to myself that after two weeks of consistently feeding and three raps on a tree about the same time every day works very well to get them out from under cover.

But again, I'll stress for their own safety and mine, I've tried to get them back further in the forest. There was a time about two years ago when they would bang on trees twenty-four hours a day. It was a nightmare for my dogs, and somewhat uncomfortable for me, as well.

I have done all of my own research and have received much ridicule for it. However, occasionally I will get a good comment on my work, and that helps keep me going. If I listened to those who want to destroy me, I would have bailed out a long time ago.

The creatures still have never harmed me, but they have scared the hell out of me more than once. I think they are just as afraid of me as I am of them. They could be afraid of my camera, scared to get too close to anything man-made. I guess after bumping into a few electric fences anything intelligent, or even dumb, would learn fast. But even through the scares, I'm still trying to accomplish something more than I've already done. I wouldn't be able to stand myself if I was to quit.

There still are many ifs. My biggest fear is that word of what I'm doing will get out in the public and some half-cocked fool will try to kill one of the beasts and drive them off my land. They don't have to live here, and their intelligence has got to be equivalent to that of a man or quite possibly superior to man. There are many thousands of acres here in the National Forest behind my home, and any little disruption that breaks the trust earned by the work that I've done could lead them to leave—I pray not.

One night around 3:00 a.m., I heard a thud by my house. I could not tell if it was the creatures or not, but most likely it was. I could smell them. Their greasy, sulfur-like smell is the most putrid smell in the world, and my dogs react wildly when they are around.

I have tried to work with others, but most are paranoid gun-toting idiots who just don't get it. How do you defend yourself against a creature who knows your intentions before you step out of the truck? It can go without detection and be up on you without your knowing it.

It, or they, showed me how easily they could have killed me with a mock attack in 1996. I was walking high on the lower watershed of McDowell, just on this lower side of the Devil's Hole, when I heard sharp bird whistles to my right. All of my attention and body posture looked in that direction. My dog began to whine and the hair stood up on his back. He jumped to the middle of the road in front of me. Then to the back of my head I heard a bang on an oak less than three feet from my head. It was a boom, not a bang. They were warning me to stay out of that area. I ran like a man running for his life. I was scared shitless and was lucky they didn't kill me and cannibalize my ass. I do believe they eat people, and in some cases I do believe they are cannibals. People go missing every year while hiking. Just check the statistics.

Forms of Communication

The creatures have several ways they apparently communicate with each other, and perhaps attempt to communicate with me. On several occasions, I have heard a loud and unusual sound coming from the woods. It sounded like something picked up a tree or log and smashed it against a tree. For a moment, I was a little afraid. They wanted me to feed them, and I didn't have anything in my house. My dogs were terrified. This noise used to send shivers through my soul, but now I realize they are giving me a signal they want something to eat. I thought about leaving a beer, but that was a dumb idea. I walked back to the house, picked up a ten-pound bag of potatoes, picked up a pocketknife, and began heading back to the mountain.

As I walked, I heard several beautiful birdlike whistles, some complex, some simple. I whistled a short five-note whistle. The other whistler imitated me perfectly. I felt a great sense of satisfaction. I felt a connection with them I hadn't felt before. I wasn't afraid.

Another time I had just got off work, I was tired, and wanted to get in my house after a long day. I walked to the door. I could hear barking on the mountain, approximately two hundred yards behind my home. It was a perfect mimic of Barney, my short-haired Beagle. Barney stood on the porch beside me, raising his ears. He was as puzzled as I was. Something was on the mountain imitating my dog. The damn things can mimic almost anything.

When I got back home one time, a strange birdlike noise came from behind my house. I stood on my deck for about seven minutes. Every time I would start in the house, the noise would start about the same time. This happened about four times over a seven-minute period. I saw nothing, but the foliage is thick behind my house. I thought it was just a bird, so I didn't pay too much attention to it, but it was a bird sound I was not familiar with. I must not forget here that I can rule out nothing and must record everything that happens: noises, shapes in the forest, movements, wind directions, odors, etc. Almost nothing can be overlooked to notice something as elusive as this creature is.

I know how to keep it close to the house all the time; all I've got to do is to take food out on a consistent basis, but I'm not going to be able to keep this up forever. Reason Number One: They drive my dogs crazy. Reason Number Two: It's somewhat annoying to me. One month, every time I would go outside, they would throw hundreds of acorns at me.

Over the years I have learned the Bigfoot in my area work in social groups. They communicate with tree banging, bird calls, and sometimes by mimicking turkeys, dogs, and even human speech. They show displeasure in people by making lots of noise—at times so much noise it can be quite confusing what signals they are trying to send. Many times in the past they have sent fear into my soul. By now my fears are only a healthy respect for their way of life and their right to survive in their natural environment. In times when they feel stressed or in danger, they beat on my house, letting me know they need help or to show displeasure with hunters or strangers they do not want around.

One pleasant day, when the weather was mild and partly cloudy, I went on a picnic with my mother up on our property. We cooked hamburgers and hot dogs. We had a nice time. The old man who I had asked about whether he had ever seen any unusual animals in the area came by, too. We all had a glass of wine and something to eat. I built a small fire near the truck. It was good, clean fun.

When we left, I urinated on the fire to put it out. Usually urination on a fire will get some kind of a response out of these Bigfoot. I came home to my house at nine o'clock that night. About seventy-five yards northwest from my house, I could hear—believe it or not—something that sounded like Indians making complex and loud bird calls. This made me feel very uneasy. I was tired and did not feel like being bothered. This kept up for about five minutes. I had had enough! I opened the back window screaming, "Go away!" very loudly. Not wanting to be bothered, I went and spent the night at my mom's. I needed my rest. They were scaring me now, and I didn't know if I should continue with this project or not.

About a week later at 8:30 a.m., I started my walk with my dogs to my mobile home cabin, which is two miles from my house. Soon I could smell a goat-like or musky animal smell close by. I kept walking down my driveway from the mountain. The smell seemed close and I could hear a faint tapping on a tree nearby. A chill ran down my spine. This is how in the past they would let me know they were hungry or would beg for food. I did not stop. I was glad this happened in a way. I knew a lot of work was left to be done, but I really wasn't sure who was being studied—them or me.

The next night, I had left two bags of bread totaling about fifty pounds in my back bedroom intending to feed the Bigfoot the next day. I really had not thought much about it at the time, when early in the morning, about 12:45 a.m., my dogs began raising hell barking, but they were afraid to leave the safety of the edge of the house. I could hear bushes rattling near the creek. I thought I could spook whatever it was by screaming.

I yelled, "Hey!" as loud as I could, walking aggressively to the edge of my deck toward the movement. As I walked, I screamed, "Hey!" again. This time a heavily built black form jumped from the high bluff on one side of the creek and missed the bank on the other side. It's about a ten or twenty-five-foot drop straight down, so when it hit, it hit real hard. It sounded like all the breath was knocked out of it. It groaned in pain.

To my amazement, the mysterious dark shape began screaming, "Hey, hey, hey, hey, hey!" It would not stop. It was mimicking me. This continued for nearly an hour along with the groaning. I couldn't sleep for the noise. Finally, I fired my rifle straight into the air to try to scare it off or get it to stop.

It didn't work. Again, I heard "Hey, hey, hey, hey!" only now it sounded like the mimicking was coming from about five different directions at once. These apes seem to be capable of mimicking anything they hear, even speech. That's why I believe they are humanlike.

More Sightings and Observations

One time I had some visitors, and as we hiked behind my property, we found many hairs hanging from trees on an old trail that goes high in the mountains. We found one weird rock formation shaped like a mini Stonehenge. We wondered about the weird rock formations. I have heard they will position rocks and hunt or lie behind them. But who knows? We found many Bigfoot tracks near the campground where they and we stayed. I fed the animals here this week for that purpose. We also found a very large cat print, several in fact. Pretty scary. These tracks were huge, and officially there are not supposed to be any large wild cats or cougars in North Carolina.

Like I said, if these monsters want you, there is no defense. I have seen the large males run. They float over the ground as quadrupeds, bipedal only when reaching or standing, twelve-foot-long, baboon-type heads, razor-curved spines, front legs moving together as well as back legs, 1,200 pounds of monstrous Neanderthal terror matted with bear fat and filth to protect itself from parasites and bugs. What a stench and what a sight! No animal or man is safe from this monster. It's up to him; not us.

If fear were my biggest enemy, I would already have left, but I believe we must face them head on in order to contain them. At the same time, I am not going to march into their camp and disrupt their day, which I think would put me in grave danger. You can fix stupid, but there is no cure for being dumb. And mind you, I know where they reside. There are at least five separate groups here. I will tell you this: they stay up high on the ridges for protection. Running the ridge tops also gives you many advantages over the bottom or middle ground, especially when stalking prey or outsmarting an adversary or enemy. You simply run the ridge tops. It pole vaults you to new mountaintops in minutes when it would take hours trying to do the same feat from lower elevations. From any other strategic location it would be nearly impossible. Plus, it might add to their ability to hide, since the higher elevations are usually too steep for humans to easily climb.

I saw another male standing beside a tree near the creek. I was above him, he had hair all over his body except for his penis.

When I walk around in these woods at night, and even in the daytime, I have some concerns, believe me. I am too far in to quit now. At first I had no idea where this project would lead me and at this time no idea when and where it will end.

I found another picture on the internet of an alleged Bigfoot. The animal almost looked sort of bird-like. The thing that stood out most were its hands. They closely resemble the arm and hand of a picture that my game cam took. In my picture you see five indentations, or fingers or claws coming from a very strange looking arm. It almost looks like a bird wing. What it really is, is unknown, but I do see some resemblance to the creature on the internet.

I wrote a letter to Dr. Joe Kennedy. He had a program on television about creation versus evolution. He believes that there is no basis whatsoever for evolution. I believe if evolution were true, a common house cat would certainly know how to operate a can opener by now.

Last night I watched a documentary on zoo gorillas. When they become excited, they will pound their chests and make as much noise as possible. The same is true if they find displeasure in a particular object or thing. Sounds a lot like what I've been experiencing on my land. Sometimes when I go to feed these unknown animals on my property, they will make so much noise it sounds as if they are trying to tear the forest down. It sounds like they are running up a tree, bending it over, then letting it go. This noise is unbelievable it's so loud.

On other occasions they will bark like dogs. From this I know they are excited. This in turn excites me, and to me this is a friendly gesture, a kind of, "Finally you're here. Where's our food?" They are imitating my dogs. They could be jealous of them. I don't know.

I went for a swim at Lake Lure, about thirty miles from my home. On my way, I noticed a large set of rock cliffs near where I live. I wonder if they are their homes.

I burned some trash and split a little firewood in my backyard. I could hear running and precision movement like a cat in the woods and foliage around me. I know how they love to watch a fire, even though they know nothing about how to make fires.

Gift Exchanges

I have had several experiences that lead me to believe the creatures are prone to engage in gift exchanges. After a hike, when I came to the end of the forest, at my gate four picked mushrooms were neatly laid out in my path: coincidence? I hardly think so. They like me. We are exchanging food. I took the mushrooms but did not eat them.

Another time in a clearing I found sixty acorns that appeared to be deliberately placed in a pile. It was the first clearing I came to when I went after a rain shower to look at the grass I had planted alongside the road to my place. From that spot I could be observed from the top of the mountain all over from almost all four sides. Maybe they knew I would be curious about the acorns and were watching me.

The week before, I had put out a very small amount of food at the end of the road, approximately six hundred yards farther down the mountain from this spot. I walked to the end of the road to make sure the wind hadn't just blown down these acorns, which were still green and should not have fallen naturally. Nowhere else on the road could I find any acorns except on this spot.

I made sure I picked up every one. There were exactly sixty of them. Last year several times after I had taken food on the mountain, there were acorns and berries arranged in neat little piles for me to find, as if waiting for me. I believe they are doing this as a gesture of friendship. I really do believe they like me. My heart went out to these creatures. When I found the acorns, they were green, not ripe. It was June and it would be fall before they could be eaten. Green acorns don't fall off trees in the middle of June. But it was all they had to give me, and they gave it to me. I don't believe they are devils or demons. Devils don't bring you gifts.

My experience is that the Bigfoot reward those who are kind to them with berries, mushrooms, wild edible plants, and in my case, feathers. These include hawk feathers, turkey feathers, and grouse feathers. These gifts from the creatures are usually left the next day near the same places where I laid out food for them and where I would be sure to find them. It makes me believe they have very human-like qualities, and it is a known fact the great apes are the only animals besides humans that engage in gift giving or exchanges.

Rob experienced the same thing one time down in Texas when he and a buddy found two entire wings from a freshly killed hawk directly on their path during a hike in dense woods. They actually heard the hawk's distress cries when it was being killed, like it was being torn apart. It was obvious something left the hawk wings where they would be sure to find them. They couldn't figure out any natural predator that could've killed that hawk, or would even want to, and thought it might be a warning from the hairy wild man. I think it was probably a gift from the wild man, kind of like a salute acknowledging them as warriors with enough balls to go into those woods and look for him.

Most of the movement I notice from the creatures occurs at night. Perhaps due to pressure from habitat loss from humans clearing forested land for residential areas and farming, these ape-men have been forced to limit their activities to nighttime. Not by choice, but simply for survival by foraging for food, they are restricted to being nocturnal, especially in areas that are marginally populated. If the ozone layer of our atmosphere were completely destroyed, we too, not by choice, but for a means of survival, would only come out at night. Daytime activities would probably cease as we know them.

After years of these experiences and observations, I recently had another encounter that helps keep me motivated in this work. I was casually making the drive to my home on the mountain up my driveway. I had just started the steep part of the road when I saw a solid black figure on all fours stand up on two feet, jump straight across the road fifteen feet in a straight line, and then jump eight feet straight up the embankment. The whole movement looked almost machine-like. The figure landed on the bank on two feet, its arms moved forward and it again assumed a four-point stance. It kept moving until it was out of sight.

I can't exactly explain how I felt. There was no fear. I was glad I got to see it. Seeing something like this only makes me want to see and know more. What I saw was like something that really didn't belong to anything we know as human beings, but with the skill and body movements it had, perhaps it really belongs here more than us. I know of no human or wildlife other than a deer that could've performed such a physical feat.

Here I want to note, I saw no facial features, no body hair—only a large black object, with the shape of a very well-defined muscular human being and the blackest black I've ever seen. He appeared to be about six to seven feet in height. His head was relatively small compared to the rest of his body size and was almost out of proportion. Again, his movements were very machine-like, and extremely fast as we understand bodily movement in human terms. I cannot describe how it feels to see and be part of something I can't easily explain. There may be no logical explanation for what is happening here.

They Travel Along the Streams

The area where I have my camera set up is only about fifteen feet from a bold stream. My theory is that they frequently travel close to the water, along creeks and rivers. I've found a lot of hair on laurel limbs near this area. Another reason I believe they travel close to running water is the different temperatures of the layers of air might help enclose their scent. The air currents along the streams could serve as a shield. Also, the movement and noise of rushing streams could help camouflage their movement. This intelligent, human-like creature could thus move for days without being detected by other, less intelligent forms of wildlife.

A stream would also serve another purpose as a food source. Fish, snakes, minnows, frogs, tadpoles, and crawfish could be plentiful. Besides these considerations, everything that drinks has eventually come to the water, which would make it the perfect place for the ultimate predator to operate from.

Tom Wonders about His Responsibilities

Today I pondered upon all the possibilities and the tremendous responsibility I have to these Yeti. Should I try to protect these animals from crazy hunters who might read this, believe it, and then try to capture or kill one? How could I protect them? It would break my heart to be responsible for the death of one of my friends. I'd hate to see one in a zoo, or the remains of one displayed in some museum.

Is the world ready to accept the fact that Bigfoot actually does exist? Would the government try to cover it up? At this point, I doubt even the Smithsonian is ready for this sort of mind-blowing reality.

Over and above that, am I ready for this? Dealing with the unknown is definitely exciting and a little scary, especially when a situation could become life threatening for me. It makes a person think. Is it worth it? For the first time in my life I feel I've found my life's true work. I have more purpose, more calling than I ever dreamed of or imagined.

There are scientists and zoologist who spend years, even lifetimes, hunting and researching these creatures and find nothing except a footprint. But me, I'm so fortunate. My home is in the corner of their backyard. I have been truly blessed. I have a sort of love for these creatures. It's a strange emotion, I can't quite explain it, but it is a good feeling. At least I know there is some trust between us. Otherwise there would be no way they would keep coming to see me.

Fear is the Greatest Obstacle

I have come to the point where I am beginning to realize how important it is for me to continue this work. I could be the only person who has this opportunity to develop a somewhat limited relationship with what I believe to be a prehistoric man—and maybe a social group of them at that. When I first started I had no idea there were so many of them.

The biggest obstacle has been trying to overcome my fear of not knowing what might happen to me. What would happen if there were a misunderstanding on their part, maybe them thinking I might want to join them for whatever reason, or even the possibility of the females thinking I want to mate? I couldn't handle it.

Here is another of my greatest fears. A dominant male might think I am encroaching on his territory or his pride, and he might try to kill me. In this case, I would be helpless because I always go into the forest unarmed: no guns and no knife. I would not be much of a match for a normal human being, much less an eight-hundred-pound Neanderthal man, heavily muscled and as agile as a mountain lion.

At least for now, I have decided to finish what I have started regardless of the outcome. If I succeed, I could be a very famous man and great wealth could be only a doorstep away, but the true reward would be the knowledge that will come from this and be shared with the world and generations to come. I may never prove this phenomenon called Bigfoot and/or *Gigantopithecus*. All I can do is share my experience and explain them as best as I can to the reader and hope it may give us all a better understanding of what is really going on.

They are very undeserving of their names that associate them with evil. Men have attached such names as Swamp Devil and Abominable Snowman to them because it's something they don't understand. One reason I believe there has been so little contact with man is when one of us sees Bigfoot, our first reaction is fear. Animals and humans react to emotions instinctively. Fear is certainly not one of our best emotions to impress, but even a child or infant reacts with fear. It is partly because of our fear, I believe, that they have avoided mankind. Maybe they seemed like devils, because on occasion they do tend to be as mean as shit and very unpredictable. Their disposition is like that of a very large gorilla who just ate a box of badass for breakfast.

I can remember when I was afraid—very afraid—of them. I would get ready to leave my home or finish doing chores around the back yard picking up sticks, raking leaves, or whatever. Just as I would start to leave, one would come crashing through the forest, wide open, making more noise than a locomotive, tearing bushes, limbs, and small trees. Yeah, I was scared. Beside that, I was forever finding dead dogs in the woods, some of them mine, torn to shreds and most of them eaten, not hardly wasting a bite.

Sometimes fear still creeps in when I dream, and I'll wake up and remember my dreams, and I'm a little scared. But for the most part, I can handle it now. I know why no man has done this kind of work for any period of time. It's because nobody's got the balls for it. People might see a Bigfoot some place in Oregon or Washington state, but right after they see it, they always haul ass, scared shitless. No one but me is dumb enough to work on this project, but I'm in a Catch-22 situation. I'm so far in, if it kills me—so be it. I'm going to finish this research regardless of the outcome. It would be a tragic shame to let what has happened here go unnoticed by the scientific community, as well as the world at large.

Most so-called researchers only report stories told to them by other people. Very few have the balls or take the time to do any real research on their own. I think some come in and do a little field work after a sighting, but you can do very little in a month, and most only spend a few hours with an observer who actually had a sighting. They are only fooling themselves. I have done a lot of my own research and have received much ridicule for it.

Again, the main problem is that many researchers and investigators start off with the idea that Bigfoot is a dangerous beast to be feared, rather than a creature that exists in nature. Civilized society is far more of a beast than this thing. We rape our forests, pollute our rivers, slaughter our unborn, all in the name of humanity. We approached the Indians the same way, though they were far more civilized than any of us. They had sacred respect for nature—they were true environmentalists. But us, we stole their land and polluted their world. We told them their religions were wrong and herded them into concentration camps we call reservations. Who is the real Devil here? It doesn't take long to figure this out. But it was the generation before us who was responsible for this. Maybe this whole thing is to make us think.

FIVE

Rob's Investigations

This chapter gives a summary of Rob's findings prior to beginning his collaboration with Tom. It covers a period of a little over twenty years beginning in 1988, and includes information and evidence gathered from his personal experiences, witness interviews, and his cooperation with other researchers. All of these investigations occurred specifically in Southeast Texas, both in the Big Thicket and in the bottomland swamps of the Sabine River bordering Louisiana.

The Creature on the Pipeline

Any follow-up research I might have done after I received a number of astonishing eyewitness reports while working at the Kountze, Texas, newspaper in 1979, which were detailed in an earlier chapter, was disrupted when a job offer obligated me to move to another part of the state near Austin. During the next few years, no doubt partly just from having been physically removed from the palpable sense of wonder that emanates from those old woods, doubts started creeping back into my mind. There had to be some kind of logical explanation for the sightings. Maybe they were cases of honest wildlife misidentifications embellished by people's imaginations. Wasn't it backward in this modern age to take such things as hairy monsters seriously?

In the fall of 1988, through another unexpected turn of fate, I found myself living back in Sour Lake teaching English for a private school in Beaumont, Texas, and being drawn once more into investigating the local mysteries. On a lark, I attended a Halloween spook house at the old school building in Saratoga in the heart of the Thicket, joined by a friend who was encouraging me to write about the local folklore. We set up a card table out front, where it was my intention to interview the revelers as they prepared for a hayride on the infamous Saratoga Ghost Road. Spectral "ghost lights" had been seen for generations on the road, and it was widely thought to be the absolute best place for a spooky Halloween experience.

A group of four curious country boys wearing boots, jeans, and western hats timidly approached our table. As I attempted to talk them into being interviewed, asking them

if they had seen anything unusual in the woods around Saratoga recently, one of the boys who called himself Buckshot
stepped forward.

"Mister, the only thing I can think of was that ape-
looking critter we saw out by the old bayou bridge when
we were squirrel hunting last year," he said, glancing at
the three other boys with him.

"All of you saw it?" I asked with more than a little surprise. I was hardly expecting a multiple-witness-encounter
report, and it looked like one was falling in my lap.

"Yes, sir," Buckshot drawled, "and he was a pretty big
ol' booger, too. We figured it must've been some kind of
escaped gorilla or chimpanzee or something." The boys all
nodded their heads in agreement. "It was fast, too, so we
didn't see him for long. 'Course, it's pretty easy to get lost
in a hurry in the palmetto flats out by the bayou."

"We might've seen it one other time from a distance
of a couple hundred yards across a pasture when we were
working cows for a rice farmer out toward Sour Lake,"
one of the other boys volunteered. "At first, we thought it
was a calf that lost sight of his momma and was wandering from the herd. But it was too big, plus it didn't move
at all like a cow and it looked way too shaggy."

The boys said they did not report the matter to the law
because they didn't think the animal would pose any threat
to anyone. I suspected without saying so the real reason
was if the boys had thought the ape-looking critter was a

potential menace, they would have wanted the adventure and glory of hunting down and bagging it for themselves.

What really surprised and excited me was that the boys' story actually supported one I had received only a short time before from an officer of the Big Thicket Association, a conservation group largely responsible for the creation of the Preserve. A lady who lived in the woods near the old oil field on the outskirts of Saratoga contacted them to say she had seen a large, hairy ape-looking thing close to her house near the reservoir in the late afternoon twilight making its way toward the bayou.

I didn't take that sighting too seriously at the time, both because I was told the woman came from a family of questionable reputation, and also because it was a secondhand account. I had not yet had a chance to interview the actual witness. Also, I wondered whether since she had seen the creature in the poor light of dusk if her imagination wasn't playing tricks on her. There was one detail, however, which did interest me.

The woman said when the ape thing became aware she was watching it and bolted into the woods, it let out a long, loud, eerie howl that sent shivers up her spine. I had only recently become aware of accounts of such howling sounds from the Bigfoot of California and the Pacific Northwest. I was not aware of this behavior having ever been reported of the Big Thicket wild man, which made it perhaps more likely the Saratoga woman's was a genuine sighting. Also, from the descriptions of the two incidents, they had occurred within no more than a few miles of each other within roughly the same time frame in 1987 or early 1988.

Over the next few months, I received more reports of fairly recent, alleged wild man sightings from several sources including my family, friends and acquaintances, the Big Thicket Association, and some of my students. The witnesses represented a random sample of people from backwoods Thicket communities like Village Mills, Saratoga, Pinewood, Bevil Oaks, and Little Rock. In every case, as far as I could tell, those involved were unaware similar creatures had been seen nearby elsewhere. I tried to pinpoint as accurately as possible on a topographical map where the incidents took place. Slowly it dawned on me there could be a pattern. They all seem to have happened near a stream, and several of them were along the watershed of Little Pine Island Bayou in Hardin County.

There could have been several reasons for this. The creatures could have been drawn to the creeks and bayous for similar reasons their human witnesses had been. They could have been looking for water, trying to catch fish and frogs, or they could have come to hunt. The woods are generally more open with less brushy undergrowth right alongside the stream banks because those areas are frequently under water. That would make it easier to spot prey and hunt for deer, wild hogs, and small game like possums and rabbits. Since humans and the mystery hominids might come to the bayous, creeks, and rivers for the same reasons, that's where I decided to concentrate my field research.

The stream corridors could also serve as pathways for the Bigfoot to move more easily through the woods. Even the hairy monsters would find the going a lot less strenuous there than having to fight their way through the virtually solid walls of yaupon, possum haw, and swamp privet all interlaced with honeysuckle, rattan, and briar vines they would run into in the Thicket's interior depths.

Then another thought hit me.

What would make it even easier for them to travel long distances in the shortest amount of time would be to follow the oil or natural gas pipeline right-of-ways that crisscross the East Texas woods. Typically, these are about fifty to seventy-five feet across, are entirely cleared of trees and brush, and are kept mowed by the pipeline companies. More than just pathways, they could act like Bigfoot superhighways where they would encounter the least possible resistance and still remain mostly hidden from humans, except for maybe fleeting glances by an occasional hunter. Despite these possible insights, I knew I would be facing nearly insurmountable odds in trying to find the creatures. When and where specifically should I go?

Then I noticed something else on the map. One of the major pipelines closely parallels the course of Little Pine Island Bayou, sometimes coming to within a few hundred yards of it, for what looked like a good twenty or thirty miles. That might be a good place to start, I thought, especially since the bayou runs through public land in the Big Thicket National Preserve and there appeared to be points on the pipeline within the Preserve's boundary. I would worry about when to go there later.

You might think having come to these realizations I would be eager to get out into the woods. No doubt I was intrigued and excited, but I struggled to work up the courage. It was apparent from what I had read and from the stories I had collected that encounters almost always occurred either right before or right after sunset, during the night, or just before dawn. From all indications, the animal is nocturnal and lives off game that keep the same hours. The odds of having an encounter would increase during their hours of peak activity. I was going to have to risk facing this thing in the dark—a dreadful prospect.

Most of the guys I grew up with, including seasoned hunters and outdoorsmen, would not want to be caught alone at night in the Thicket, even if they were armed to the teeth—whether or not they knew anything about the wild man stories. It is an intimidating environment even in the daytime, and I knew I would have to test my theories at night. Eventually, I resigned myself to the inevitability of consequences. I just had to trust my fate. I would never overcome my fears. It was simply a case of curiosity outweighing them. My need to know was stronger than my need to be safe.

It's hard to explain how I knew when to go. It just hit me. I had already scouted out a place I could enter the Preserve and follow the bayou to where it intersects the pipeline. I got there after about an hour's hike from my car, allowing plenty of time to cross the deep, steep-banked sloughs that feed into the bayou, and be able to set up my modest camp before nightfall. Another advantage of being on the pipeline was that its straightness gave me an unobstructed line of sight as far as I could see in two directions, which was all the better for the prospects of a sighting.

My equipment included a machete, binoculars, a rain poncho, and a spotlight-style flashlight. It was my intention to travel light and keep an all-night vigil, but I also brought a pup tent and a sleeping bag just in case. Turns out, it wasn't difficult to stay awake. The cacophony of loud swamp noises from frogs, insects, birds, and an occasional yelping coyote was impossible to tune out. I made sure to bring repellant, but mosquitoes buzzing around my head all light, even if they wouldn't bite me, added to my discomfort. Of course, a heightened sense of alertness and anticipation added to my wakefulness.

I set up the tent in the middle of the right-of-way for shelter in case it started raining, unsnapped the poncho, rolled it out on the ground as a tarpaulin, used the sleeping bag as a pillow, and lay back to gaze at the stars, wait, and listen. It would be hard for anything as large as a Bigfoot to approach me from any direction without making enough noise to alert me. If it did, it would soon have a strong beam from my high-powered spotlight glaring in its eyes. From what I had read, that would probably be enough to scare it off, but hopefully not before I got a good look at it.

That thought gave me some comfort, but I was startled nonetheless several times during the night from noises that turned out to be false alarms from armadillos, possums, and raccoons. As the night progressed, heavy dew began to form on everything, adding to the miserable conditions. There was a deer stand nearby that would get me off the ground and in drier conditions. It wasn't hunting season, so I decided the owner surely wouldn't mind if I borrowed his stand for just part of one night.

By the time I got situated on the deer stand, sitting with my legs hanging off the side, it was about 3:00 a.m. and I was getting pretty tired. It got harder and harder to stay awake, and I dozed off a couple of times. About two hours later, an hour or so before sunrise, something woke me up with a start. At first, I heard nothing but absolute dead silence, and then I was overwhelmed with a blast of sound I could never have dreamed of or thought possible.

It was obviously an animal's howl, but the volume was louder than a fire truck's siren or a freight train's whistle, only deeper in tone and more resonant. It was so loud the ringing in my ears was painful, and I could feel sound waves reverberating in my chest cavity. Immediately I thought of the Saratoga woman who claimed she had heard a howling, hairy, upright walking beast. This had to be it or one like it. My theory had been correct. It had showed up, and from the sound of it, it had to be close by. I suspected it was no farther away than the other side of the pipeline, within twenty or twenty-five yards from me.

By then the moon had set and the woods were pitch black. I reached for my spotlight and aimed it straight across the open space of the right-of-way. To my horror the batteries had drained. I must have left the switch on one of the times I dozed off. All it would produce now was a feeble glimmer. The howl went on for what seemed an impossible duration with bizarre undulations and pitch changes. There was no doubt the beast knew I was there. Instinctively, I knew its howl was directed at me, and I could not tell what the monster intended. I had no defense against it. It could tear my head off if it wanted.

Strangely, I did not react out of fear, as terrifying as I could have taken the circumstances to be. A strange calm overcame me. I took a firm grip on the handle of my machete and hollered as loud as I could.

"All right, you old booger! You're here, and I know you see me! It's your move!"

I sat as still as possible. Trying to escape would have been useless. It was so dark I could barely see my hand in front of my face and would have only stumbled blindly through the swampy muck, an easy prey for the wild man. At any instant, the thing could pounce upon me. That harsh reality kept me alert as I peered into the inky black, my sense of hearing heightened. The howl slowly faded away, its echoes bouncing around in the woods eerily. Then, just as suddenly as it had arrived, the mysterious creature went away with sounds of its shuffling through the clutter on the forest floor and the rustling of palmetto fronds and the underbrush announcing its departure.

I was both relieved and disappointed. Apparently the great beast meant me no harm, but I did not get to see it. Slowly, I came down from my adrenaline rush. Within an hour the morning dawned, and it was light enough to go check out the area the howling seemed to come from. The ground clutter from leaves, twigs, and branches was too thick for it to have left any tracks. Given all the information I had collected, there was no doubt what had howled at me. Nothing but a very large animal could produce a sound that loud and long, and it definitely had an indescribable primate quality.

I was left to wonder why the wild man had spared me, and also why it had revealed itself by howling at me. It could easily have slipped by me in the dark by staying just inside the tree line on the other side of the pipeline. I could only guess it wanted me to know of its presence. Whether it meant to acknowledge and encourage my desire to learn more about it, or warn me to go no further, I could not tell.

The Devil on the Bayou

After I was introduced to outdoors expert and journalist Chester Moore on the Don Briscoe radio show, we met at a book signing I did that same weekend in Beaumont and compared notes. I could tell his momma raised him right. He was a true southern gentleman. Although we did not agree on all aspects of the wild man mystery, in particular its having any relation to the ghost lights, he was respectful of my views. For him, Bigfoot is simply an undiscovered species of normal wildlife and has no psychic or paranormal abilities. We agreed no one is truly an expert on the subject. Since nobody has produced a Bigfoot for scientific study, we don't really know for sure what it is we are dealing with.

A few weeks later, Chester sent me a copy of his book, *Bigfoot South: Examining Cryptozoology's Greatest Mystery in the Southern United States.* Our independent studies and field investigations, along with our respective knowledge of stories and legends stretching all the way from East Texas to Virginia, had led both of us to conclude there is a population of large, hairy, ape-like creatures native to the woods of the Deep South. On the inside cover he scribbled an offer, which I gladly accepted, for us to join forces and to cooperate in our further research.

Chester followed up sending me his book not long after that with an urgent phone call.

A reader of his regular outdoors newspaper column for the *Orange Leader* and *Port Arthur News* had called him with information Chester thought deserved an immediate follow-up. He has a reputation among his readers as someone they can report unusual wildlife sightings to who will listen to them and not skeptically dismiss their accounts. This particular reader said he had seen something unusual in a nearby swamp off the Sabine River. He had gone bass fishing in a channel cut into the swamp nearly a hundred years ago by loggers to reach the virgin bald cypresses for harvest.

To his surprise, he was suddenly confronted with something big, hairy, and black noisily swimming across the cut. The fisherman assumed it was a wild hog. Feral hogs, or razorbacks as they are called throughout the South, are abundant in the East Texas woods and river bottoms.

When the animal reached shore, however, its witness was shocked to realize whatever the creature was, it could not have been a hog. The thing stood upright like a man, climbed hand over hand up the steep bank, and disappeared into thick woods. And then there was the howl—an eerie, long, drawn out unearthly sound. The almost human wailing pierced the air and was so unimaginably loud it left the startled fisherman knowing this was no ordinary animal. This was an encounter with something unknown.

From a preliminary investigation of the site, Chester found out that other people had also heard the howling. There were also reports of suspicious tracks along the muddy banks that he, an acknowledged expert on animal tracks, wanted to examine closer and possibly cast. He urged me to join him and his dad, Chester, Sr., in a further examination of the area, and his tone was urgent. There had been considerable activity at the spot for at least a few weeks, and there was no telling how long it would last.

We suspected if the animals are migratory, the swamps and bayous along the Texas/Louisiana Gulf Coast might be their wintering grounds and the southern extent of their range. Visibility is also best during the wintertime in the woods when the foliage is down, so we decided to make this one of several trips to the swamp and surrounding woods before spring. I asked Miles Lewis, the editor of *Austin Para-Times* magazine at the time, who had an interest in documenting our research, to join us.

Chester and his flat-bottomed boat were already waiting for us at the dock when Miles and I turned into the parking lot of the marina on the east side of Orange. The night before, an early January Texas "norther" had pushed all the way through to the Gulf Coast and the Louisiana border. Temperatures were predicted to be in the low twenties overnight. It was seriously cold. The wetland's humidity added daggers to the blustery winds, and the bald cypresses and water tupelos surrounding us in every direction did little to shield us.

After loading our gear into Chester's boat, we cautiously made our way out into a man-made channel cut between the bayou and the river. The going was slow. We were close enough to Sabine Lake, the estuary that opens onto the Gulf, that the waters were still tidal. Despite the cold and the wind, and the obstacle of shallow water the low tide presented, it was a gloriously sunny day and our spirits were high in anticipation of adventure.

Miles commented on how unusual it had seemed to him at first that a Bigfoot would be seen so close to a pretty good-sized population center. But it didn't take him long to realize civilization receded pretty damn quick the further we got into the swamp. We had gone no more than a few hundred yards before we were in territory accessible to people only by boat.

"We're just on the margins of the swamp here," Chester responded. "People in places like Houston and Dallas and Austin who spend all their lives in the big cities and on the interstate highways between them have no clue what this country is like or what the extent of it is."

I agreed with Chester on one point. In the swampy environment of East Texas it would be possible for even a large animal, if clever enough, to so avoid detection that its very existence would be doubted. Logically, just from a consideration of available habitat and food supply, there would also be no reason to ascribe any extraordinary abilities to the creatures for their ability to sustain themselves.

"But Chester," I said, practically yelling to be heard over the din of the boat motor, "I still think there's something weird about these animals. I've had some experiences I haven't told you about. People report strange things to me, too, and I don't think they're being superstitious."

I reminded him of our conversation on the radio show and about the weird energy and power outages often associated with both wild man sightings and ghost light appearances.

A mischievous twinkle in Chester's eyes hinted maybe there were some things he hadn't told me yet either.

"Did you happen to notice the name of my boat?"

I had not noticed.

"Swamp Devil," he said.

I couldn't quite understand him.

"Swamp Devil!" he repeated a little louder.

"Well, now, that's interesting," I laughed. "That's what some of the Cajuns call them, you know. You must've been holding out on me with all this dyed in the wool flesh-and-blooder bullshit."

"What do you mean? What do the Cajuns call them?" he asked.

"Devils. They call them devils," I answered. "The legend is when the hairy monsters are seen swimming in the bayous, all of a sudden things like engine failures on the Cajuns' fishing boats start happening for no apparent reason."

Chester knew the term *loup garoux* (werewolf), but he did not know the Cajuns sometimes refer to the creatures as devils. Somehow the similarity to the name he gave his boat was spooky for me, a little too much of a coincidence.

"The Cajun word for devil is *diable*," I yelled, with strong emphasis on the last word.

No sooner had the word left my mouth, than it seemed like someone flipped a switch. The steady drone of the outboard motor suddenly shut off, a plume of thick black smoke streaming from it. The abrupt silence seemed surreal. As I watched Chester's reaction, looking back and forth between me and the motor with an astonished look on his face, the whole scene took on a dream-like quality. This could not be happening. I had just reminded Chester that mysterious engine failures are often part of Bigfoot sightings, and—Boom!

It seemed like the only thing the weird, hairy bastards were waiting for was for someone to loudly say what the Cajuns call them. It was like they wanted to impress upon us, "You boys are dealing with something weird here, and now you're in our waters. Are you sure you want to mess with us?"

Miles and I sat quietly, saying nothing as Chester tried to restart the motor. He looked at us with a sheepish expression on his face, as if he thought he owed us an apology, or at least an explanation.

"I swear this motor was running great. I've never had any problems with it before."

Not only would it not restart, the motor was frozen up, completely ruined.

There was nothing we could do but head back for the marina. There was no way we could make any headway upstream to the camp Chester's dad had set up without the outboard motor. The river's current and the north wind were too strong. There were only two oars in the boat, and being the old man in the group, I got to supervise while Chester and Miles paddled. Chester had his cell phone with him and called his friend, Bubba Hogan, in Orange to come help us. The plan was for Bubba to meet us, load our gear into his boat, take us to the camp where Chester's dad was waiting, and allow us to use his boat for the rest of the trip. We had about an hour and a half to kill before he could get there, so we paddled down current to the bulkhead of a power line tower on the river bank, tied off the boat, and got out to do a little exploring.

We decided to see if we could find any tracks or other signs of possible Bigfoot activity in the mud flats and reeds of a nearby marshy area. The going was very slow. We had to step very carefully on dead reeds where they had fallen and matted up, because the exposed mud would not support much weight. No more than twenty yards from where we started, I stepped a little too far from the reed mat and in an instant was buried up to my butt in thick mud.

It's a good thing Miles and Chester were there, because I'm not sure I would have been able to get out by myself. This is a good example of why it's not a good idea to go out in the swamp alone. It soon became obvious an animal as massive as a Bigfoot could not get through the marsh, so we went back to the boat and waited for Bubba.

It was a good time for us to reflect on the day's events, particularly the strange breakdown of the outboard motor. I didn't want to pass off the experience as a mere oddity. I had a hunch to do so would not only be missing out on an opportunity for discovery, it might also be putting us at risk.

"Boys," I said, "I hope y'all don't think what happened back there was a coincidence. Remember, I've been saying this kind of blackout is reported to me with wild man sightings pretty often, and it's exactly what I've heard the Cajuns say happens to them. That's why I think there must be some kind of energy disturbance involved."

Nobody knew what to say. If this had been a coincidence, it was one hell of one. It almost seemed orchestrated, like we were set up, and that added to the dream-like sense of unreality which overwhelmed me. I felt like an actor in a movie, and someone else had written the script and was directing the scene.

"They can't explain how the *loup garoux* does these things," I went on, "so they attribute it to witchcraft or the supernatural and call them devils. But the point is this is not mere superstition. They have real, unexplained experiences and real sightings."

"Well, I don't know if they are the same as the *loup garoux*," Chester responded, "but I have had reports of hairy, man-shaped animals seen swimming in the waters around here lately. That's one reason we're here—to investigate those sightings."

"Exactly," I said, "and we get here and the same kind of thing that sometimes happens to the Cajun fishermen happens to us. I don't mind telling you when that motor went out on us right after I said *diable*, I started seriously checking out the water around us."

We all laughed at the thought. I pointed out the creatures are frequently seen along creeks and rivers, and I had one report of witnesses who saw one swimming across the Trinity River near Dayton, Texas. This is consistent with the observations of cryptozoologists and Bigfoot hunters across the country.

With Bubba's help, we finally made it to the campsite where Chester's dad was waiting for us. We soon learned Bubba eliminated the confusion of distinguishing between Chester and his father in conversation by referring to Chester, Sr. as Pops. Pops comes from good Cajun stock, and has passed on to his son that unique cultural trait of being at home in the swamplands. I thanked them both again for inviting Miles and me on this expedition, and let them know I considered it a privilege to be there in the swamp with them.

"Miles, you know what I love about this country down here?" I kidded. "There are creatures in these woods, not even counting the wild man, that can tear you apart elbow from asshole if you happen to be in the wrong place at the wrong time or take a wrong step. You have to be on your toes. You can't take your safety for granted. Makes me feel alive."

Pops grinned and seemed pleased I obviously relished the primordial beauty and wildness of our surroundings. From the look on his face it was obvious Miles was wondering how we could love a place full of vile and hostile creatures.

"Miles," I said, "I'm grateful to the cougars, alligators, water moccasins, copperheads, and such—even to the mosquitoes. They help keep the Thicket and the swamps wild enough so a wild man could inhabit them. If this country was all nice and pretty and pleasant, we'd be overrun with shopping malls and subdivisions and there'd be no place for the wild man to live."

Chester immediately gave Miles and me a few beginner lessons on identifying tracks. He pointed out armadillo and raccoon tracks, which are the most common in the swamplands. Then he showed us how to tell the difference between deer tracks and feral hog tracks.

"This palmetto flat is virtually identical to habitat in Florida where the Myakka ape or skunk ape has been seen and reportedly photographed. It's also typical of vast regions of bottomlands and swamps along the Gulf Coast from Texas through South Louisiana and on into Florida," Chester informed us. "I think there's a good chance that the animals bed down among the palmettos, because it gives them a natural early detection warning system if anyone is approaching them."

He illustrated his point by walking a short distance. The interlacing of the palmettos' fronds created a virtual solid wall, and it was impossible to avoid brushing up against them and creating a noisy ruckus.

"As you can see, visibility is limited to only a few feet in a palmetto flat of mature plants. And they could easily hear you coming from a lot farther off than that. It would be virtually impossible to sneak up on them. Also, frequently the ground litter in a palmetto flat is not conducive to leaving clear tracks for a large animal. In places where it is clear enough, it is usually so muddy that whatever tracks are made are indistinct and hard to identify. It would be difficult, if not impossible, to track them in a place like this."

"That makes good sense to me, Chester," I responded. "These animals are not stupid. I suspect they're smart enough to have figured all of this out and to also walk where they won't leave tracks when possible. I think you may have hit on some good reasons why they are so elusive."

We made our way back to the camp and waited on Pops to return. Chester wanted to go out further into the swamp by boat to a high bluff on the banks of one of the channels cut by the bald cypress loggers so many years ago. From reports he had received, he thought there was a good chance we might pick up some prints in that particular area. On the way there we stopped where a slough emptied into the other side of the channel. It provided a large exposed muddy area that would likely yield prints if the creature had passed through there.

Chester quickly found some prints, but they were not clear due to surrounding ground clutter and leaves. What aroused his curiosity about them, however, was the stride of the steps indicated by the spacing of the tracks. We measured it at close to five feet. The normal walking stride of a fully grown man is usually less than three feet.

"The only way a man's stride would be that long would be if he were running," Chester said, "and if anyone was running through this mud, the prints would show a sliding effect, which these clearly don't."

Encouraged by this discovery, we crossed the channel to the high bank and worked back toward where another slough cut through the bank on that side. Chester explained the animals might well like to use these sloughs to travel between these cut channels and bayous because the water was shallower than in the main channels. They could walk the sloughs and not have to expend so much energy swimming.

Sure enough, we found another set of tracks. We could clearly discern where the animal had walked for about fifty feet. The stride was roughly the same as the tracks we found on the other bank, but these tracks were much more distinct. At one point, we found where the animal had stopped. Right next to each other were two prints, a left foot and a right foot.

While Pops was busy mixing the quick-setting plaster-like substance used to cast prints, Chester explained to us why he thought these were not likely to be human footprints.

"These prints are still fresh," he pointed out. "I'd say they were made within the last few hours. When the casts are ready, they should show quite a bit of detail. Notice how deep the prints are and compare the depth to your own prints."

The suspected Bigfoot prints were well over an inch and a half deep. Chester and I both weigh over two hundred pounds and the tracks we made wearing our rubber boots standing right next to the animal's tracks were less than half as deep. We even tried jumping up and down and could not make prints as deep. From the depth of the prints and the length of the stride, Chester deduced that the animal in question weighed well over three hundred pounds and was probably between six and a half and seven feet tall.

The stuff Pops used hardened in a little over half an hour. We removed the casts from the ground and washed them off. Chester was right. There was quite a bit of detail. Contours on the cast showed the impressions of the ball of the foot, the arch, and the heel. The ground had been too muddy to make out much detail on the toes, but you could see where the animal pushed off on its toes when it made a stride. It was obvious that the print was made by a bare foot. Our boot prints looked entirely different. They were flat with no contours and clearly showed a line separating the front of the boot and the heel.

To the casual observer, however, it still could have been a human foot that made these tracks. They didn't look anything like what I had come to expect of a Bigfoot print from pictures I had seen. For one thing, they weren't unimaginably large for a human to have made them. They were only about twelve inches long. Typical Bigfoot prints average fifteen to eighteen inches.

There were, however, some tracks that measured about fifteen inches found along Slop Jar Slough in Hardin County in 1980. Buddy Moore, my old boss at the *Kountze News* ran a picture and wrote a story about them in his paper. They were found by a couple of ladies who were picking may haws in a bay gall thicket. Slop Jar Slough was also where the wild man sighting reported by the *Kountze News* in August 1952 took place. It's only a few miles from Bragg Road.

A park ranger told me he saw some tracks along a slough off Village Creek with a stride longer than a man would make. Both of these accounts fit the pattern of what we were looking at—it appeared something that made large, human-like footprints had a stride longer than the tallest of men and liked walking the sloughs barefoot.

Chester said he had also cast some prints in the Southeast Texas woods in the fifteen-inch range and pointed out if all the prints were fifteen to eighteen inches long, that would be suspicious in itself.

"If Bigfoot is a real breeding animal living in these woods, it has to grow to those optimum sizes. We should expect to find some prints which are smaller. A range of sizes argues for the reality of the animals, not against it," he convincingly argued. "You have to take all the evidence together; the depth of the prints, the length of the stride, and the location. Look around you. You can only get to this place after a lengthy boat ride. Who do you think is going to be wandering around here barefoot in freezing weather?"

"If it's not some kind of a Bigfoot creature that made these prints, I guess it would have to be one seriously drunk, three-hundred-and-fifty-pound, seven-foot tall ol' Cajun boy," I cracked. "And I guess he would also have to know where we were going to look for tracks so he could leave some there to fool us."

"Right," Chester cracked back with mock sarcasm, "and he would also have to have a serious foot deformity. Take a closer look at this print. Notice that the heel is very narrow at the back and is elongated. Notice also how the outside of the foot has an accentuated curve from where the little toe should be to the big toe, suggestive of a foot that is much more bow shaped than a typical human foot. This is typical of other prints I've found along with what look like baby prints. In my opinion, this is the print of an unknown primate, a female. They are smaller and more bowed out than the males' prints."

That night we cruised the swamp with sophisticated electronic equipment. We had parabolic sound amplifiers to try to pick up the slightest unusual sound. We had third-generation night-vision scopes. Chester also employed the age-old hunting method of calling game. He imitated the loud whoop said to be one of several vocalizations the animals make along with the eerie and unbelievably loud howl for which they are better known. Sometimes the animals are said to answer back. That night we were not so lucky.

After a couple of hours of neither hearing nor seeing anything unusual, we gave up and returned to camp. We gathered for a short time around a large fire Pops built, but it proved inadequate to fight off the by then bitter cold. I retired to my tent for the night to bundle up in my sleeping bag. Chester and Miles stayed up late. The next morning they said they heard a suspicious howl briefly in the wee hours not long before dawn.

With Chester's help we had literally picked up the creatures' trail of footprints. The circumstances surrounding the breakdown of the outboard, especially in the context of the Cajun traditions convinced me we had also picked up another trail.

Six

Why It's So Hard to Prove Their Existence

Are They Trying to Avoid Us?

If Bigfoot sightings are as frequent and widely distributed across this continent as the surprising number of eyewitness encounters currently being reported would make it seem, why has there not been enough evidence gathered to prove beyond any doubt that they even exist? After more than fifty years of research, objective evidence verified by reputable authorities to be from unknown primates amounts to no more than a small number of castings of footprints and a few hair samples.

Why should it be so difficult to prove the existence of a physically real animal? There are several factors that could contribute to the present lack of definitive proof. Could it be that our scientific knowledge of the world is not as complete as we would like to think? Maybe Bigfoot simply chooses to avoid humans, and for reasons some may find disturbing, is stealthy enough to do so very effectively.

It's not hard to understand why they would want nothing to do with us. They probably have no use for the way we live, or they might fear the consequences of contact with us, such as the threat of disease. The possibility of contracting viral or bacterial illnesses similar to the way Native American populations suffered from Old World pandemic diseases after Europeans arrived. They might be avoiding us out of simple self-preservation. It would be such a waste for us to infect them out of our ignorance.

They apparently have survived despite centuries of mankind's relentless attack on the wilderness for timber, coal, oil, uranium, and a warehouse of other minerals and natural resources we use to make our lives a little easier. Maybe they have the intelligence to stay away from what they see as the destructiveness of humans. They know from experience and observation it's best to leave us alone. That could be why they live in seclusion away from the biggest predator of all—man. Perhaps they have learned from the examples of the wolf and the mountain lion. We nearly hunted them to extinction. Only until this century have we learned the value of having these wonderful animals around. Sadly, we seem to have a lot to learn to know what to do with the Bigfoot if we ever do have contact with them in any sustained and meaningful way.

Although many hunters have reported sightings and thereby have contributed substantially to what little knowledge we have of the creatures, in some cases and in some places hunting activity can present a problem to any sort of serious observation efforts. As Tom points out of his section of the Smoky Mountains:

> "It's hard as hell to do any kind of experimentation or study in the woods when you got a bunch of half-witted idiots plundering the forest looking for something to shoot or steal. In a way, I wish Bigfoot would just beat the crap out of one of them, or maybe just scare the hell out of them, or both. He's certainly scared the shit out of me a number of times, and I rarely ever carry a gun. Chief Two Trees in Old Fort told me they hate guns, that they were shy and only trusted a few people."

Given such motivations, how does something as big, hairy, loud and stinky as an ape-man remain virtually hidden from humans except for a fleeting glance or a short-lived chance encounter?

Camouflage Experts?

To attempt to solve this conundrum, we believe it is essential Bigfoot not be considered mere dumb animals helplessly awaiting the inevitability of being shot and killed by humans as the only means of validating their existence. From our field notes and observations, we hope to demonstrate they could have extraordinary camouflaging abilities derived from a high degree of intelligence and keen instincts. Moreover, there could be facets of this ability that go beyond the present common-sense understanding of human psychology and sensory perception.

Camouflage serves two purposes in nature. One is defensive. The intended prey blends in with its surroundings in order to hide from would-be predators. The other is offensive. The predator blends in with its surroundings in order to stalk its prey and to get close enough when it attacks so its prey will not have time to escape. Motionlessness is a key aspect of camouflaging. A rabbit sitting perfectly still against a backdrop of weeds and bushes is very difficult to see, even for the sharpest eyes. As a lion stalks an antelope in the African savanna, the coloration of its coat makes it almost invisible against the background of high grass that hides its approach. The lion moves very slowly, stopping frequently until it gets into springing distance.

It's interesting to speculate what would have happened to the squirrel hunter at the Texas Bigfoot conference who told Rob the story of his sighting if he had taken one more step toward the oak tree. That Bigfoot might not have been sleeping; it might have been using the background of the tree to hide itself, staying perfectly still while the hunter approached so it would visually blend in with the tree and be difficult to see for any prospective prey. Of course, the hunter might have come across a Bigfoot hunting squirrels, just like he was, rather than trying to bag a homo sapien, or it might have been keeping still defensively like a rabbit, hoping to not be seen by the approaching human.

The fact that Bigfoot feed on wild hogs and deer, which seem to be their preferred prey, raises a question we would pose to hunters. Grover Krantz observed there is no evidence Bigfoot use or are capable of using tools of any kind. This is one reason he thought the creatures are more animal than human. If they don't use tools, which would include traps, spears, clubs, or any type of projectile, how do they catch their prey? There is considerable evidence they actually kill deer and hogs with their bare hands by breaking their necks, gutting them, or by grabbing them by one or more legs and slamming them against trees. Here's the question: How do they get close enough to deer or wild hogs to be able to catch them bare-handed?

Both of these animals are swift of foot and have keen senses of smell and hearing. Nature has designed them to be wary and alert. That's why human hunters who pursue them have hunting blinds, because it would otherwise be difficult to even see either of these animals in the woods, much less get close enough to grab one. You could spend years in thick woods typical of suspected southern Bigfoot habitat and only rarely ever see a deer. It is more common to see feral hogs. Their habit of rooting and creating mud wallows along the creeks and bayous and river bottoms leaves them a little more exposed. But just let anyone try to get any closer than about twenty yards from either a deer or a wild hog. It would just about be impossible. With that much of a head start, it's unlikely a Bigfoot could simply run one down. So how do the Bigfoot get close enough to catch their preferred prey without using tools, weapons, or projectiles?

In some cases it may simply involve Bigfoot's exhibiting an unexpected cleverness. A classic sighting report from the files of the Gulf Coast Bigfoot Research Organization's database illustrates this point.

....

The sighting took place in the Blue Ridge Mountains of North Carolina in Tom's neck of the woods in the late 1800s. The story was handed down to the person who submitted it by his great grandmother. She was a full-blooded Cherokee and this happened to her when she was thirteen years old. She was gathering food along a creek bank in a deep hollow in the mountains. She heard gunshots up on the ridge and then heard someone running down the side of the hill toward her from the direction of the shots. She hid herself in the bushes to avoid being involved in whatever trouble was going on.

To her surprise, what emerged from the woods was not a man, but a seven-foot-tall, hairy creature covered with light reddish brown hair. Its hair was much longer on the head and shoulders than on the rest of its body. She recognized it immediately as a male *nun yunu wi*, which means Stone Coat or Stone Man, one of the Cherokee names for the Bigfoot creatures. The creature hurriedly found a pile of brush and debris alongside the creek. It lay down next to the pile and quickly covered itself with leaves, branches, and dirt until it was completely hidden from its pursuers.

It is conceivable a Bigfoot might conceal itself in a similar way alongside a worn game path or near a frequently used watering hole to get the jump on a deer or a wild hog. A similar technique is used by Special Forces military snipers who wear what are called "ghillie" suits.

Ghillie suits are camouflage jumpsuits with hundreds of long, shredded strands of stripped burlap or a similar material which completely covers them, including a hood. They enable the sniper to stand, sit, or lie down motionless in brush and ground litter in a way which renders them virtually invisible. It almost seems that the actions of the North Carolina Bigfoot were more human-like than animal-like in the thought-out and calculated way it concealed itself, but it could have been acting instinctively. Nature might have designed Bigfoot's long, shaggy hair to serve a similar purpose to the ghillie suit. Indeed, a good-sized man wearing a ghillie suit seen from even a short distance in heavy woods bears a striking resemblance to a hominid with long, shaggy hair.

From decades of personal experience in the North Carolina woods Tom offers these interesting observations about Bigfoot's apparent camouflaging ability:

"These creatures are black, and black is a tough color to see in the woods. This is a real problem when it comes to trying to photograph them. Black is a camouflage color. Look at the military tanks. They are painted in black, green, and brown. I see how Mother Nature has provided perfectly for the Bigfoot. He blends in perfectly with the foliage. No wonder he's rarely ever spotted. All he would have to do is stoop down and be perfectly still and to our eyes he would look like a burned-out tree stump. They are completely capable of being right on top of you before you can ever see them. How they use the landscape and trees to move without detection is unreal."

The variation of colors reported of Bigfoot is paralleled by the fact ghillie suits are customized, dyed, and assembled to blend in with diverse color scheme backgrounds of particular localized areas. Hence, the coloration of a Bigfoot from the mountains of North Carolina might differ from that of a Bigfoot from the swamps of Louisiana or East

Texas. The fact these color differences are reported by witnesses, in fact, probably lends credibility to their reports.

Problems with Research Strategies?

Yet another reason for the lack of definitive proof of Bigfoot's existence stems from the strategies researchers consistently employ to look for them. The groups we have had contact with utilize what amounts to a quasi-militaristic, invade-and-conquer tactic. Many go into the wild with all kinds of high-tech cameras and sophisticated technology hoping to gather evidence in a manner as scientifically objective as possible, but they are also armed to the teeth with guns powerful enough to take down a charging bull elephant. If what we will consider later about projected intentionality and the mystery hominids' sensitivity to it are accurate, the researchers apparently hostile intentions would make encountering the creatures very unlikely.

The wild hairy hominids would easily make themselves scarce at the first sign of such blatant obtrusiveness, even if those who violated their territorial boundaries were not bearing weapons. If they are as intelligent as we hope this narrative will demonstrate, and if they have a sense of humor, they might even think the efforts of all those clambering to be the first to "discover" them to be almost laughable.

"Another problem with the self-styled professional Bigfoot research groups," Tom pointed out, "is they go into an area for just a few days, set up their game cams, and then leave after a few days. It took me two years of constant battery changing, camera checking, and food placement to get anything really considered viable photographic evidence; not to mention the twenty-year period since I had my first encounter."

In a typical Bigfoot investigation, a reputable person—if he or she is not afraid of possible public ridicule—will report a seemingly authentic sighting to the authorities. Upon investigation, sometimes within only a few hours, no Bigfoot is to be found. In rarer cases, investigative organizations might send a group to an area that has had a spate of recent sightings, or even a long history of sightings, only to have the same outcome—no Bigfoot are present. Then, instead of maintaining a presence where there has been recent activity, they go on to where the next suspected sightings have been reported—and get the same lack of results.

It is little wonder so many organized research efforts get such scant rewards, considering they last for only a few days or even a few hours at a stretch. This constitutes another major reason why there is a dearth of definitive proof for Bigfoot's existence. As Tom puts it:

> "Most researchers would never continue to do this
> work in one place for a week, much less many years.
> I became obsessed with trying to find out what
> the Bigfoot are exactly, and wanted to understand
> what they're doing and their mode of operation.
> This has certainly produced more questions than

answers. It is simply my hardheadedness up here in the mountains and Rob's down there in the swamps that make us a good team. We simply refuse to give up, regardless of not having an explanation for the Bigfoot at this point. Both of us have seen and experienced too much in our own backyards to quit now or to move on to other places."

What is called for is sustained, long-term—preferably permanent—investigation in highly localized areas with long histories of repeated sightings right up to present times like in the Pisgah National Forest and the Big Thicket National Preserve. We feel that in this regard our research methodology has much to offer. Tom's unique living situation fits the bill for this approach perfectly. Unlike most of us, he doesn't have to leave the scene of the action to return to pushing pencils, turning knobs, stroking keyboards, or whatever it takes to survive these days. In fact, he doesn't have to leave the scene at all—he lives in it.

Even as we write, Rob is entering retirement and is making arrangements to put himself in a similar position in the specific area of the Big Thicket where he has done literally decades of research work and where there continue to be hairy wild man sightings. That puts us both in position to be at the core of the prototype for future Bigfoot research wherein we will continue and concentrate our attempts to build an atmosphere of mutual respect in which the creatures might accept, or at least tolerate and hopefully be curious about, a human presence.

Repeatability of Research Results

Lack of the repeated finding of identical or very similar evidence under controlled conditions is a serious problem with mystery hairy hominid research. This is a major reason for the lack of scientifically acceptable definitive proof, since that insists on consistent experimental results in the laboratory to validate a hypothesis. Unfortunately, Bigfoot does not seem ready to respond to investigators' entreaties to show up on demand or to voluntarily submit to an exam in a lab anytime soon. If a Bigfoot is spotted in a particular area and even an immediate investigation fails to turn one up, however, it does not mean the witness was mistaken, delusional, lying, or that his testimony is worthless, as skeptics are prone to conclude. It just means it is difficult to duplicate the evidence.

Any experienced outdoors person, camper, or hunter who spends time in the wilderness knows, you could go into the woods where there is a known population of a particular wildlife species, like the coyote for example, and you could spend days there and never see one. You might hear one howling in the night; you might find telltale tracks—both of which have been reported of suspected Bigfoot encounters—but you might never actually see one, much less have the briefest opportunity to photograph one or enable someone else to see it.

If their presence were not widely accepted, without a good photograph you might have no real conclusive evidence that even something as common as coyotes still inhabited the area. If it were not generally acknowledged by experts they were present in a given area, even having one or two good photographs might not offer enough proof.

Due to the huge popularity of digital cameras, motion-sensitive game trail cams, and cell phones, there has been a proliferation of photos allegedly of giant, hairy mystery hominids. In virtually every case, unfortunately, the images are not clear enough to constitute serious evidence. Moreover, with the development of computer enhancement of digital images, it is getting harder and harder to prove anything with photographs. Beyond that is the difficulty of being able to repeat getting similar photos.

Some time back Chester Moore, the previously cited East Texas wildlife expert, found tracks and heard howls of what he suspected were red wolves. The red wolf (*Canis rufus*), is thought to have long been extirpated from its original range in East Texas because of predation by humans, loss of habitat, and having been absorbed into interbreeding with coyotes to produce a hybrid population that has lost its common wolf-like characteristics. Populations of pure-blood red wolves are said to no longer exist there. It was somewhat surprising, then, that Chester actually was able to obtain several photographs with a game trail camera of a large, dog-like animal that does have those wolfish indicators.

Even with his photographs, Chester has had difficulty proving his case that red wolves are still in Southeast Texas. If critics accuse him of some kind of trickery using an old photo, it would be difficult for him to defend himself. The animals could be so rare it would be almost impossible for him or anyone else to reproduce the same photographic results. This does not negate the significance of the images he has, it only illustrates the difficulty of proving the existence of animals in the wild with photographs.

This is another example of the need for long-term research. If a continuing presence were maintained in a given locale, enough photographs of the animal in question might be taken by enough different people or be taken enough different times by the same person to begin to constitute acceptable evidence on the basis of the reproducibility of results.

Being able to get similar photographs consistently in the same locale is one of the goals we have set for our continued research. Hopefully, proceeds from the sale of this book will enable us to afford the out-of-pocket expenses needed for the time and equipment necessary to produce viable results.

One might object and say the examples of coyotes and red wolves are different from the situation with Bigfoot in this very important respect. Coyotes are known to actually exist and red wolves are known to have at least existed in the recent past. If Bigfoot were a real species of higher primate, it would almost certainly have already been discovered by now, with or without recent photos. This demonstrably may not be the case.

In June 2006, *British Science Weekly* reported a population of large primates previously known as the Bondo Mystery Ape from its existence having not been scientifically confirmed, had been observed by a team from the University of Amsterdam in the Bili Forest in the Democratic Republic of the Congo. It has a mixture of traits of both gorillas and chimpanzees, but its range of behavior is different from both. Pending further studies to determine its taxonomic classification, it could be classified as a new subspecies of chimp or gorilla, a rare hybrid of the two, or even a distinct species of great ape. If this can be the case with great apes, who's to say there could not also be mystery hominids whose existence has not been officially confirmed, particularly if they are as intelligent as humans and have an extraordinary ability to remain hidden?

If what we are dealing with in the Bigfoot phenomenon is not just an undiscovered primate, but an almost human creature of high intelligence and intuitive sensitivity, the hit-and-miss efforts which are now most commonly employed will not be adequate. Someone needs to be in a position to have enough prolonged contact with the creatures to develop a relationship of mutual trust. Tom may be the only person to have accomplished that to any significant degree and to have documented his efforts both with his writing and with photographs.

Why Can't We Track Them Down?

Having been raised in the rural South, we were both taught at an early age to respect the hunting and tracking skills of the traditional backwoodsman. As has been noted, we take sightings reports from hunters very seriously. Most of them know when they are seeing or hearing something truly out of the ordinary—they are in the woods where many of them have hunted for decades and where their families may have hunted for generations. They also tend to be very down-to-earth personality types and not the kind subject to airy-fairy flights of imagination. This being the case, we would like to pose a question to experienced hunters.

Why can't we track down a Bigfoot? Yes, we are convinced their trails can be picked up and followed for some distance and the trails may remain intact for some duration, but why can't we track one down? If these things are as big and smelly as they are alleged to be, they would leave tracks even an amateur could follow, and they should leave a scent trail a good bloodhound could follow for weeks. Why, then, do their trails often seem to just disappear or to grow cold within days or sometimes within only a few hours?

Typically a Bigfoot will show up in a given location where witnesses may experience a repulsive musky odor, and may also hear loud, ear-splitting howls or screams. It may leave footprints, will be seen by a number of persons over a period of a few days, and will then simply vanish. In some reported cases, search parties have been formed within only a few hours of a sighting. These frequently have involved trained local law enforcement officials, and especially in the South where hunting with dogs is a traditional practice, dogs have sometimes been used in the searches.

Without exception, these efforts have yielded negative results, sometimes after large areas have been searched for days at a time. Tracks may be found, but their trail ends without leading to a Bigfoot. Very rarely one or more of the party may actually see the animal, but they have never been able to catch up with one. What gives here? How do these creatures remain so elusive, much more so than would be expected of even the craftiest, most cunning known animal? If they are real, solid, flesh-and-blood animals, how can we account for their sudden disappearing acts and for the problem of not actually being able to find one, except for rare, brief, inconclusive glimpses? Are we left to assume they must be shapeshifters, dimension jumpers, or phantoms?

Do Dogs Provide a Clue?

An important and little recognized clue to understanding this mystery, as well as a source of validation for the reality of the creatures' existence, may lie in the antipathy the creatures seem to have for dogs and in the abject terror with which dogs regard Bigfoot.

An experienced dog handler in the old Southern hunting tradition, Tom has seen his dogs react in a puzzling manner to the beasts. Some dogs that would aggressively pursue both bears and mountain lions without hesitation would cower, whimper, and hide under the porch when they heard the eerie howls of the unknown hairy creatures in the nearby woods or smelled their putrid scent on the wind.

Tom's greatest fears were confirmed when some of his dogs went missing and he found their remains in the woods around his home, the bones picked clean of flesh and only the paws not eaten. In several subsequent, apparently mock attacks, he didn't know whether the beasts would charge him and tear him apart limb from limb just as they had his prized dogs, or if they just intended to warn him off their territory.

Rob was told this story which further illustrates the point about how dogs regard Bigfoot with fear, by a caller during one of his appearances on the Art Bell show.

The caller, who could not give his name for security reasons, said he was a soldier stationed at a large army base in North Carolina. He was an MP assigned the duty of patrolling the base's perimeter during the late-night and pre-dawn hours. Part of the base extends well out into a heavily forested and hilly area where one night while on patrol he came across a dog. The dog seemed disturbed. It was howling, growling, and acting very strangely. It occurred to the solider the dog might be rabid and he couldn't tell whether it had seen him or not and whether it was a threat to attack him.

Just as he was trying to make a decision on what to do about the dog, "a huge ape-like animal jumped down from a tree, grabbed that dog, broke its back, and literally tore it apart ripping its legs off in front of my eyes," he said. The ape either did not see the solider or paid him no mind and vanished quickly into the darkness of the surrounding woods.

But why would the huge ape kill the dog? By all accounts dogs are terrified of Bigfoot. Research files are brimming with accounts of dogs slinking away in fear from encounters with Bigfoot, with the hair on their backs sticking straight up and their tails tucked between their legs, wanting no part of the beasts. Cases of dogs being eaten by Bigfoot seem to be the exception rather than the rule. Could there be another reason Bigfoot would kill them?

Grover Krantz commented in his book, *Big Footprints: A Scientific Inquiry into the Reality of Sasquatch*, "dogs are universally reported to be terrified when in the vicinity of a sasquatch. This has long been reported by the major writers, and I have run across dozens of such reports myself." He goes on to point out the sasquatch does not even need to be in sight for dogs to react to sound, smells, tracks, or any other evidence that a sasquatch might be close by. Furthermore, he writes, "this fear is common to all breeds of dogs, of both sexes—from ratters to bear hunters, from lap dogs to bloodhounds. Even the most devoted companion dogs have refused to follow their masters in the direction of one of these animals." Krantz speculates further that the frantic fear reaction of dogs to Bigfoot might be produced by a pheromone contained in the stench the creatures are known to project.

Apparently the poor dog on the army base was drawn to the treed ape out of instinctive curiosity. Its bizarre behavior likely came as a result of it picking up the creature's scent, and it could not get away fast enough when it realized too late it had caught up with more than it could handle. But if the dog was reacting out of fear and it posed no threat to the ape in the tree, why would the ape kill the dog? Again, Krantz offers some insight.

He notes that "there are many stories of sasquatches going out of their way to kill dogs," even though as he says, "the largest dog would pose no threat to any sasquatch beyond infancy." Why, then, would any Bigfoot go out of its way to kill dogs, if dogs pose no physical threat? Krantz speculates, "there must be some conflict between these two species that has no obvious significance at our present state of knowledge."

This conflict between dogs and Bigfoot might not be obvious if we consider dogs only within the context of their most common modern functions as pets and companions of humans and participants in those ridiculous dog shows. But the relationship between dogs and humans is an ancient one. Dogs were one of the first animals to be domesticated. Until very recent times dogs served more utilitarian purposes in their relationship with mankind than they do today. From time immemorial we have put them on watch to guard our domiciles, villages, and barnyards, and they have been helpers in tending herds of sheep, goats, and cattle.

Could it be because of the relationship dogs have with human beings that Bigfoot go out of their way to kill dogs? It's easy to imagine a Bigfoot would not want a dog to give away its presence if it wanted to make a quick meal from the easy pickings of a herd of domesticated livestock. Is it because dogs would alarm humans to their presence that they go out of their way to dispose of dogs?

There is one other function dogs have traditionally served for humans that might be a clue of an even subtler source of the Bigfoot's antipathy toward them. From ancient times dogs have helped hunters track down and flush out game. It was noted earlier how many a posse or search party has gone out in hot pursuit of a Bigfoot only to come up empty-handed. In more than a few documented cases, these organized searches set out with packs of trained hunting dogs or police bloodhounds. These searches have a consistent pattern in which some of the dogs would refuse to follow the trail, others would quickly come back, but were completely cowed, and some would not come back at all, or were later found to have been literally torn apart. But in every case the dogs lost the Bigfoot's trail and the Bigfoot simply vanished. Or did it?

Perhaps it vanished to human eyes but not to dog eyes, and that is the reason Bigfoot make the extra effort to do away with dogs. A dog's sense of smell is known to be far more sensitive than a human's, and a dog can hear frequencies of sound inaudible to us. Perhaps this applies to sight, as well. Dogs may be able to see the creatures even when they are undetectable by human sight. Or dogs also may not be able to see them, but with their acute senses of smell and hearing, they know the Bigfoot are there even when they cannot see them. In either case, this may be what freaks dogs out so much about Bigfoot. A confrontation with Bigfoot is a confusing contradiction of sensory input for dogs and sends them into panic.

Tom's experiences with a number of his own dogs independently corroborates Krantz's observations and constitutes serious objective evidence that he is dealing with an unknown predator on both his property and his adjoining neighbors' land. Dogs supposedly do not have imaginations like human beings and are not subject to deluding themselves about what their keen senses tell them. For this reason, the reaction of dogs is probably a better indicator of the reality of mystery primates than human perception is.

The following first-person accounts from Tom's field notes document his observations regarding his dogs over a period of several years and what he came to conclude from them:

Today I walked the same trip as last week and they snuck up behind me, whistling like birds, shaking trees, and throwing one large rock. My dogs became terrified and so did I.

I heard a muffled sound, almost like a radio transmission over a walkie-talkie. My dogs went crazy. I have never heard such a noise. I was a little afraid. My dogs were spooked and so was I, a bit. I went inside and slept next to a gun. If it ever tries to come in the house, I swear I will shoot it. I hate to say this, but it's true. Again, things are getting weird.

When I come home from work, it seems I can almost always hear something on the mountain shaking a rhododendron or banging on a big tree. This has happened almost every night for a week. My dogs go crazy when they hear it.

Last night, I lay on my deck and my dogs began to bark. I could hear brush shuffling and trees being bent and let go on the mountain. This is always such a strange sound and it's also a bit frightening, because you never know when you're going to hear it. My dogs are at a loss when they hear it, because they react with a stupor. They don't really seem to know what to do.

One day I found a small black Labrador retriever puppy about nine weeks old beside the main highway. Somebody had put him out. He was as cute as a button, and I am a sucker for abandoned dogs. I put him in a small cage under the backside of my home for safekeeping when I got home. I laid down on a couch in my living room and began to fall asleep. I always let Junior, my black Chow, sleep near me in my den. About 5:30 a.m., Junior bolted and began to bark. Half awake, I opened the sliding glass doors and sicced my dog on whatever it was.

He attacked and I heard a high-pitched scream, like a horse whinnying but with the vocal strength of a lion's roar. I was terrified and could not go back to sleep. Junior ran back up the stairs to my deck and pawed the sliding glass doors wanting in. My dog was scared shitless, and so was I.

The next day, I built a dog pen around three oak trees in my backyard and put a doghouse by one of the older trees. I put the small dog there, thinking it would surely be safe.

About 4:30 the next morning I heard a large tree crashing down, part of it hitting the front of my house. I jumped out of bed screaming and ran outside. A huge black form ran across the back yard and into the creek. A huge oak laid on top of the doghouse, the fence was torn down, and part of the tree laid on my front porch. My black Lab was gone, and I never saw him again.

Once on a hike with my dog, Peanut, I could hear sharp, bird-like calls coming from the surrounding woods and brush. Peanut ran to my side with fear. It was unusual to see a one-hundred-pound Chow scared, coming to my side. Again, I heard the piercing bird-like calls. I was five miles from any other human beings. My dog began to whine and whimper with panic. I just told him it was okay and reached down to pet him.

I never saw anything but the rock cliffs and hemlocks that surrounded the roads. Before I had a chance to look around real good, I heard a sound like someone had taken a tree and started banging on it with another one. The noise was so loud that fear overcame me. I had to reach to the bottom of my soul to figure out what to do next.

I started running wide open screaming, "One, two, three, four, five, six, seven, eight, nine, ten!" I ran all the way to an open field about three miles down the mountain, repeating my military cadence over and over again. Why I hollered in repetition I don't know. I outran my dog home. I could've beaten Jesse Owens that day. That day was tough.

When I reflect back, I ran and hollered out loud subconsciously to try and muffle the real fear that had completely engulfed my being. It was my way of trying to cover up my real emotions. I know that day Bigfoot knew that they had my number. They might have just wanted something to eat. In the past this had been a common reaction from them, but the whole ordeal completely caught me off guard. Besides that, the damned thing crept up on me sneaky-like.

If I had a little food or maybe planned things out better, maybe I wouldn't have run, but I did. I ran like a rabbit from a fox! Through all this time, my dogs are still frightened of them, and probably rightfully so. I believe they kill and eat canines. I've lost enough of them to at least prove something enjoys dog meat on this mountain. The life expectancy of a mean dog here on my place averages about twenty-six months. That's not so great.

Last week my dog Peanut disappeared. It was during a heavy rain, almost a flood. The next day footprints were all around my house. I really am getting pissed about my dogs disappearing. There seems to be no end to it, but what in the hell can I do? I really loved that dog. He was one of my best friends. My heart felt emotions rip through my soul. God damn it, they had better quit killing my fucking dogs. Who knows, maybe I'm next?

Junior weighed seventy-five pounds, wasn't scared of anything, and could be as mean as hell. On Thanksgiving Day, 1991 my faithful companion disappeared. I cried like a baby. I loved that dog. To put it honestly, I am still scared to death when I think about what happened to him. I went through the horrible emotion of finding pieces of my beloved dog torn to shreds in the woods—and yes, I have very mixed emotions of what's going on here.

My neighbor, who is basically a shy man, who never really communicates much with anybody, told me that he had also lost three dogs, not really

knowing what had happened to them. I decided
to pick his brain a little for information. I had just
finished writing a small article for a newspaper
about my first encounter I had had with the "man/
apes," or whatever the hell they really are.

I handed my friend the article. When he finished
reading it he said, "Tommy, I was cutting wood here
about three months ago and when I looked up on the
mountain by your house, I saw a huge black form. It
was standing, leaning over a bit, with arms that reached
to its knees. I watched it for about five minutes. It
wasn't a bear or a man, but it sure as hell watched me
cut my firewood. I looked up again and it was gone."

I told him, "Mister, that's where your dog went."

He nodded in agreement. He was now a
believer. I asked him if he had ever smelled
anything in the evening after dark that smelled like
rotten potatoes, or anything that smelled that bad.

"What an awful stench!" he said.

He continued and told me about finding his little
beagle, Snoopy, who loved to roam the mountains
and woods behind our homes, and Snoopy was torn
to pieces. All that was left of him was a small piece
of his leg, with some hair intact, and what little was
left of the leg bone had all of the marrow sucked out.
His voiced continued to quiver and he cried. He put
his hand on my shoulder and said, "Tommy, to be
perfectly honest with you, I am afraid."

In my mind, I know they are real because I've seen them with my own two eyes. My dogs know they are real because they are very much afraid of them. That's all the proof I need for myself, but for the rest of the world, who aren't here to see how my dogs react or don't understand dogs, I need solid, concrete evidence. Even then there will still be room for doubt.

I have experienced hearing tree banging, weird, bird-like whistles, and dog killings. Yeah, they used to love to eat my dogs, or at least I thought they did. Let's put it this way: something got rid of a lot of dogs around here and would eat everything except their feet. Maybe it was wolves or mountain lions, but I don't think so. Those animals run from dogs, and dogs aren't afraid of them. My dogs are terrified of these monsters. I haven't physically seen them eating a dog. I pray that I never do. That would be a little too much for me. You could just take me to the psycho ward. At that point, it would be hard to handle.

Despite the fact most large breeds of dogs are not afraid of any wildlife known to be native to North America, there is no doubt that something in the North Carolina Smoky Mountains terrorizes them and sends them into an uncharacteristic panic. Cases of dogs being eaten by Bigfoot seem to be the exception rather than the rule. Could there be another reason Bigfoot would kill them?

The Bigfoot's ability to apparently vanish might well result from their employing an extraordinary means of camouflaging themselves beyond those we have already considered, which makes them even less vulnerable to human detection. And the reason they have such a sense of urgency to destroy dogs is dogs can either see through their camouflage or use other senses to detect the Bigfoot's presence. Although dogs may not pose a direct threat, they give away Bigfoot's location to the only other animal that poses any significant threat to the ancient, hairy creatures—Man.

Do They Hide in Our Blind Spots?

All of us like to think we live in the real world and see the world as it really is. This notion, however, is illusory. Habit is a big component of perception. To a large extent we see what we expect to see, and sometimes we can be blind to something we don't expect to see. Experiments have demonstrated that this habit can prevent you from seeing what is literally right in front of your face.

The now-famous experiment, originally conducted by university psychology professors Daniel Simons and Christopher Chabris and described in their book, *Invisible Gorilla: And Other Ways Our Intuition Deceive Us*, illustrates what is known as inattentional blindness. Volunteers tested are shown a short video (less than a minute long) of two teams of people moving to and fro and throwing a basketball around.

Test subjects are asked to follow the path of the basketball, whether bounced or thrown through the air, from player to player and to concentrate on silently counting to themselves only those passes made among people wearing white, ignoring passes made among people wearing black. Halfway through the video a female student dressed in a full-body gorilla suit walks among the players, stops in the middle of them, beats her chest like a gorilla would, and then walks off having spent about nine seconds on the screen.

Test subjects are first asked how many passes they counted. The correct number is irrelevant. What is amazing is that when asked if they noticed anyone other than the players in the video, about half confessed they did not notice anything and did not see the gorilla at all. The experiment has been conducted many times in different conditions, among diverse people and in different countries with the same results—about half the participants not seeing the gorilla. How could they not see something so obvious? What made the gorilla invisible to them when it stood still and looked directly at them? The professors say this error of perception comes from a lack of attention having been paid to an unexpected object. They conclude:

> "When people devote their attention to a particular
> area or aspect of their visual world, they tend not
> to notice unexpected objects, even when those

unexpected objects are salient, potentially important, and appear right where they are looking. In other words, the subjects were concentrating so hard on counting the passes they were 'blind' to the gorilla right in front of their eyes."

When an unsuspecting Rob took the test, he did not see the gorilla. However, he was faintly aware of a slight blur moving across the screen, which temporarily interrupted his counting the passes. We naturally take a lot of ribbing from friends and acquaintances who think we are naïve and horribly unsophisticated to even entertain the possibility that Bigfoot actually exists. One such friend viewed the video and failed to see the Invisible Gorilla.

At first the skeptic thought it somehow illustrated the obvious fact that Bigfoot sightings are no more than optical illusions. We were quick to point out to him it is more likely the exact opposite is the case. The video shows how something as extraordinary as a hairy ape could literally be right in front of you, and there's a 50 percent chance you wouldn't see it, particularly if your attention was otherwise engaged and you were not expecting to see it.

This may help explain why Bigfoot are sometimes visible and sometimes not visible and show how a person's psychological habits can form a blind spot. The fact the mystery creatures can vanish seemingly at will, however, implies there is something else at play. It might be a Bigfoot is somehow capable of locating a potential witness's blind spot and hiding in it.

Precisely this ability is claimed of expert trackers in various Native American shamanic traditions, and is based on the perception that all creatures are creatures of habit. Ancient Apache scouts, according to wilderness survival expert, Tom Brown, Jr., for example, had the ability to observe their intended prey or enemies to determine their habitual psychological ruts in whatever were their everyday routines. They would then accordingly position themselves, be so silent and so still as to stop their brain activity, and blend so thoroughly into the background as to become virtually invisible to their victims.

The Apache trackers' skills, Brown wrote in *The Tracker*, were judged by how close they could come to their prey before making the kill. The best were said to be able to actually touch the luckless animal or human they were tracking before they would be even be seen by it.

Bigfoot's having or not having this type of mysterious mental capacity is not a matter of mere speculation. It is based on actual field observations of otherwise inexplicable events associated with wild mystery hominids. All of this leads to a conclusion that most Bigfoot researchers find very uncomfortable. Bigfoot appears to be psychic—and that gives them a decided advantage in remaining hidden.

SEVEN

Does Bigfoot Have Psychic or Paranormal Powers?

Before we two reluctant but determined investigators met and began to compare our research findings, each of us independently had bizarre experiences that would be difficult to explain without at least considering the spooky hypothesis that Bigfoot has unusual mental powers. This is way more than speculation for us—it is a theory based on verifiable findings directly resulting from our field work.

In this section, we recount some of those incidents in our own words quoted directly from our respective notes. We certainly are not the only ones who are having such experiences and making these claims about Bigfoot's mysterious powers. Brief references to the observations of other Bigfoot researchers and to cutting-edge psychical research from Europe back up ours being genuinely psychic events.

Rob's Visit to the Health Food Store

Earlier I told the story about Chester Moore's boat motor breaking down in the middle of the Sabine River at the precise instant I loudly hollered *diable*, the French word for the Bigfoot-type swamp devils said to dwell in the Louisiana bayou county. I've always thought that bizarre turn of events should not be passed off as just a coincidence. It very well could have been an example of the creatures exerting the peculiar power of mysteriously causing machinery and equipment malfunctions when the hairy monsters are spotted swimming in their local bayou waters. This skill was first attributed to them by Cajun shrimpers and fishermen. I had already experienced another amazing sequence of synchronistic events, also possibly involving the creatures, which was even harder to dismiss and would make their ability to disrupt electrical or mechanical devices seem like child's play.

A few days before I was to appear on Art Bell's *Coast to Coast* radio show, I received an e-mail from a gentleman from Baytown, Texas, who had seen the promotions on Art's website. He identified himself as John Bounds and said he owns a camp house in East Texas in Polk County near the Alabama-Coushatta Indian reservation. For thirty years or so, he claims to have had many experiences with Bigfoot-like creatures there, and said he would be listening to the show with interest. He sent his phone number, so I called to thank him for his good wishes. He gave a few more details about his land and said he had a friend who lives near Austin who would back up his story.

A few weeks after the show, I was driving through Austin on the way to see some friends. My route went by a health food store where I sometimes shop, and I suddenly got a strong urge to go in. It wasn't that I needed to buy anything. Something told me there was someone there I needed to see. I have learned to pay attention to such hunches, so I pulled into the parking lot and went in. Right away I ran into Randy Ward, an old friend I hadn't seen in some time, who was there grocery shopping.

Randy and I exchanged warm greetings and he began to ask me about my first book, which had just been published. This was enough of a coincidence to make me think somehow I had been picking up that Randy was in the store. As we talked, I noticed a dark-haired, slender man in the same aisle who seemed to be eavesdropping.

He seemed genuinely interested in our topic of conversation and totally unconcerned about being inconspicuous, as he edged closer and closer to Randy and me. Finally, he walked right up to me, almost as if confronting me, and asked, "Mister, are you talking about Bigfoot in the Big Thicket?"

I replied, a little startled at his boldness, that, indeed, that was what we were talking about.

"Well, if you want to know about that, you can ask me, because I've seen Bigfoot there," he brashly declared.

"How close were you to them?" I asked, figuring there was no harm in going along with him, as he might even be telling the truth.

"Just as close as I am to you right now," he said, looking me straight in the eye. He went on tell how he had a friend who owned a camp up in East Texas and that they frequently went there. For him, the place was like a spiritual retreat, as he went there for the peace and solitude and to practice meditation. He said the property had a hammock set up near an extensive natural bower formed of entangled vines and tree boughs. He liked to go there and lie in the hammock and meditate.

Sometimes, when he entered a profound state of peace-fulness, he said, the hairy forest people would become curious about him, and would come right up to the hammock and lean over and watch him. He was never afraid of them, he said, because he felt he had an understanding with the crea-tures that he meant them no harm and shared their love of the woods. This was all beginning to sound strangely familiar.

"Wait a minute. Where is your friend's camp located?" I asked, struggling to remember the name of the gentleman who had e-mailed me.

"It's in the Big Thicket, all right," the stranger answered, as if I were questioning that point. "It's in Polk County, near the Indian reservation."

"John Bounds!" I exclaimed, as much to myself in amazement as to the stranger, as the name clicked into conscious memory. "You're talking about John Bounds!" I said, still excited, my mind totally blown away by this extraordinary turn of events. "You must be the friend he talked about who lives near Austin who could verify his Bigfoot sightings."

The conversation suddenly took on a different tone. The stranger's confrontational attitude softened. His mind was as blown as mine was that I should already know about the place he was trying to describe to me and already knew the name of his friend who owned the camp house. Randy sensed something extraordinary was happening and graciously went on his way.

We introduced ourselves. The man's name was Ron Patillo. He wanted to discuss the matter further and invited me to join him for a cup of coffee. Ron questioned me about my interest in Bigfoot research, almost as if he were testing me out of an interest in protecting what he imagined were the interests of the Bigfoot.

"Let me tell you something," he said. "These creatures are psychic. If you go in there with guns with the intent to shoot one to prove that they exist, you'll never see one. They'll pick up on you before you even get there. If you want to see them, you need someone like me to help you, who also has psychic ability."

I decided I would be the judge of that, but I suspected there was some truth in what he was saying. Ron went on to tell me at one time he had been a professional psychic counselor back in Orange, Texas. Eventually, he had to give up the profession, he said, because it was too physically and mentally taxing. Ron seemed to grow more and more comfortable with my intentions toward the creatures as we continued our discussion. I thanked him for his time and assured him I appreciated his perspective regarding the creatures.

Just as we were about to end our conversation, Ron abruptly asked me, "Are you psychic?"

"I guess that depends on how you define psychic," I answered. "I don't make any effort to cultivate psychic ability, but sometimes strange things do happen. What would you call what happened between us just now? I meet my friend Randy here on a hunch, by coincidence you happen to be here at the same time we are and overhear our conversation, and you turn out to be the very person John Bounds told me about. I mean, are you going to say that was no more than an incredible string of coincidences, or would you say there was something psychic to it?"

"Yes, I guess you could say it was a psychic event." Ron answered.

"Well, in this case I guess I'm psychic," I said, "but no more than you or Randy, and I can't help but think this whole experience confirms what you said about the hairy forest people. Maybe they're the ones who are really the psychics here. It almost seems like our meeting each other was orchestrated by someone else. If Randy hadn't been here and you hadn't overheard our conversation, we would not have met. Is it possible to psychically influence the flow of events in some way? And why would anyone do that?

In this case, it seems like the intent was to forcefully and dramatically deliver the message that to deal with these creatures we had better be prepared to learn some subtle things about the nature of our own minds. And if they weren't the ones who sent the message, then who was it who sent it on their behalf? It's like my old friend Bill says: 'Whose mind is it anyway?'"

When I told Chester about that unlikely string of events right after his boat motor froze up for no apparent reason in the middle of the Sabine River, things got even more bizarre. He was clearly a little uncomfortable with what I was suggesting, so I quickly reassured him.

"I'm not saying these beings are morally or mentally superior to us or they're infallible in any way or the Bigfoot equivalent of UFO space brothers or anything of the type. Like you, I suspect they are more animal than human and are physical like us, but they could have some mental capabilities that we might once have had in common with them that most of us no longer have."

"I don't know about that," Chester responded, "but I can tell you this. The camp you were talking about in Polk County..."

"Yeah...," I said, interrupting him as I caught his drift. "Don't tell me you know about that place!"

"Not only do I know about it, I've been there," he assured me. "There are all kinds of Bigfoot signs there. Prints, limb breaks, vocalizations, the works. There's no doubt in my mind. They're on that land all right. At least some of the time they're on it."

It turns out Chester had been introduced to John Bounds by Bobby Hamilton of the Gulf Coast Bigfoot Research Organization. Bounds had notified the group of the activity on his land and volunteered to let them conduct research. Chester had to admit that, although this might be more an example of the tight-knit small world of Texas Bigfoot hunters than an example of psychic connectedness, the string of coincidences I encountered in Austin with Ron extended to him as well.

"This may well further illustrate my point," I said. "We may all be connected to each other in subtle ways we do not normally experience. We could also potentially be consciously connected to nature in a profound way that we have lost somehow, perhaps out of cultural conditioning, but that the wild man has not lost. And that's a good reason it is so hard for us to find them, and why we could have so much to gain by learning about them and their extraordinary abilities."

Mind Pictures and "Headspeak"

As far-out as Bigfoot having psychic powers might seem, and as much as all categories of psychic phenomena are pooh-poohed in mainstream scientific and academic circles in the United States, there has been considerable legitimate institutional research done on telepathy in Europe. More to the point, much of the research that could have a direct bearing on the Bigfoot enigma has been done specifically on telepathy between animals and humans.

In England, Professor Rupert Sheldrake presents considerable evidence in *Dogs That Know When Their Owners Are Coming Home,* that indicates there may be a strong psychic connection between pets and their owners that statistically cannot be accounted for within the current scientific paradigm.

Examples include such things as dogs sitting expectantly at the door to indicate they know when their masters are coming home even at unexpected or unscheduled times; and cats who consistently and inconveniently disappear just when their owners are about to take them to the vet. If you've ever owned a dog or a cat, you've probably had similar experiences.

It is common to think of telepathy as the direct, mind-to-mind transfer of thoughts composed of words from one person to another. Sheldrake has suggested it might be better to think of the contents of telepathic communication as intentionality rather than thoughts, composed of pictures or images rather than words. He thinks it is its owner's intentionality that is being picked up by dogs and cats, sometimes before their owners have even visualized their intentions or put them into words in their minds, and with or without the owners being present.

Similar powers may have atrophied in humans due to lack of use as we now enjoy many new forms of communication in this modern age of electronic information. They may also have disappeared because, as Sheldrake says, such powers are, "not cultivated in our educational system," and are "not only ignored but often denied."

He further reasons, "If domestic animals are telepathic with their human owners, then it seems likely that animals are telepathic with each other, and that this may play an important part in the wild." Something like telepathy could be involved in the coordination of flocks of birds in flight where thousands of birds move in split-second syncopation that could not logically be the result of ordinary communication. Examples of mammals with such ability include the coordinated movement of herd animals and members of a wolf pack.

In so many words, telepathy among animals is probably the norm, not the exception. Bigfoot most likely has this particular psychic ability, and maybe others as well, refined to a degree we humans can scarcely imagine. Since Bigfoot is likely to be our closest genetic relative, there is a strong possibility that meaningful, extended contact with them could help human beings regain our lost telepathic powers.

Khat Hansen, a Choctaw medicine woman who claims to have telepathic communications with the Sasquatch, gave us a very compelling perspective on how it works.

"They are very simple in speech type and tend to use 'headspeak' or mind pictures to speak with humans," she told us. Beyond that, she said if we ever wanted to consciously communicate with them using this "headspeak," we would have to gain their trust.

"It has taken me a lifetime," she said.

This is clearly a matter of having pure intentions when it comes to the welfare of the hairy ones and of learning how to receptively look at the pictures in one's mind. Tom's experience in field research has led him to similar conclusions:

I know from my experience these creatures respond to our inner psyches. They are quiet when I am quiet. When I don't beat on trees, they don't beat on trees unless they are upset about something or someone. These beings are three steps ahead of us. They can hide or disappear at will. They know our intentions before we step out of our truck in the forest. They can also go without detection and be right on top of you with ease. If they have hostile intentions, we have no defense against them.

Many times since I have started my research, I have had numerous researchers ask me to try to communicate with the Bigfoot telepathically. They

are believed to be quite psychic, and according to
Indian folklore, even to have the ability to read
your mind. I believe ancient man may have had
the ability to read your bodily features, the type of
posture you are holding, and your facial features very
quickly. From this they could intuit your attitude and
intentions very quickly that come out in the way you
conduct yourself whether in the woods, or in public.
I believe the Bigfoot to be experts in this area, and
that is one reason why so few professional Bigfooters
ever come up with anything substantial.

Many of these professionals carry weapons
and the big hairy people realize that very quickly,
warning the others quickly to the presence of the
invaders with tree beats and so on. They work
in social groups, according to my experience, or
they very much appear to do so. I think they post
guards to alert others when there is danger.

But back to the question at hand: Are the
sasquatches psychic? I am not one of those people
who on a regular basis try to sell their thoughts to the
Bigfoot. However, when I would go to feed them in
the woods by my house, they would jump and make
tons of noise to let me know they were there. The
tremendous amount of noise was quite disturbing to
me and almost put my mind into a state of panic. So
I tried to communicate that to them telepathically,

and they eventually quit making noise when I would go to feed them. Now the only time they make noise is when they want me to know of their presence or if they show displeasure in something. So, yes, I would say they are very much psychic in a sense.

The only other time I set out to communicate with them, I spoke out loud in the area where my trail cameras are set up and asked them to please reveal themselves to my cameras so I could help them. Strangely enough, I got no physical sasquatch, but the next day my camera was full of pictures of orb-like lights. What do such orbs have to do with Bigfoot? Much research is still needed in this area, but the work I am doing with Rob Riggs certainly raises that question.

I refuse to go out into the woods and try to project thoughts and hopefully get answers telepathically in my mind from a monster that may or may not even exist. One reason is that I believe the subconscious mind will answer the questions we have for us by placing little voices in our heads. To me, this is sort of where we enter into the world of the nut cases who chase the hairy ones and hear all kind of things in their heads from the Bigfoot.

However, I still respect the opinions of those who claim this to be true (many in the Bigfoot world do) whether or not such telepathic communication is a reality. I am afraid I would start hearing voices all the time and need to seek a professional for medication. But just seeing one is reason for checking the sanity charts, much less hearing voices or seeing mind pictures. So this is a practice I have never used, nor will I try to.

There are many stories that say the Bigfoot can and do read your mind for up to five miles when nearing their territory. Personally, I think they have a finely attuned sense of awareness, which gives them an edge that we simply do not have as human beings. I take pictures of coyotes on my game cams, but I have never seen one, but that does mean that they are not there. They, too, are finely attuned to their surroundings, just as the Bigfoot are.

It has taken me twenty years to get only a handful of pictures as evidence. If they are so finely attuned with their senses, maybe they are quite psychic, and that's why it's hard to ever produce any results. The new technology has aided me well, as I am able to produce thousands of pictures in the span of a month with the spy cameras. Most of the photos have to be discarded even though I get bobcats, coyotes, deer, turkeys, bears, you name it. If it's wild, we get it.

No doubt it is annoying to advocates of the flesh-and-blood approach to Bigfoot research who think the beasts are just an undiscovered but otherwise normal animal, but such a mind-to-mind link would almost have to be called telepathic or psychic in nature. As we have seen, the question of whether the beasts have such uncanny abilities cannot be dismissed just so the flesh-and-blooders can have a tidy research model that does not threaten their comfortable scientific-materialistic worldview.

Tom pretty well sums up the frustration of those of us who have become aware of this particularly confusing aspect of the mystery hairy primate enigma:

> The problem that most of us have with this strange creature is that God made it, or evolution made it, with a much greater sense of depth of how to use the world around it to its own advantage than we have. Human beings cannot understand a being that appears—and that you can see—and then apparently disappears into thin air. I have been a witness to this, although I do not understand how and why it works. I just accept it as a reality.

How Would Bigfoot's Psychic Powers Work?

There have been extensive studies done in the former USSR and Czechoslovakia of telepathy among animals, and between animals and humans. The findings could shed light on the matter of Bigfoot's alleged mental powers, as well as possibly on the energy medium in which they occur.

In *Strange Secrets: Real Government Files on the Unknown,*
Nick Redfern and Andy Roberts report on recently declassi-
fied files from British, American, and former Soviet government research into various aspects of extra sensory perception. Government-funded research in ESP, especially during
the Cold War, was mostly intended to determine whether
there were any practical applications in espionage. Soviet research included that of B. S. Kazhinskiy, who in 1962 advanced the theory that, "animals are capable of visual and
aural perception and reflex understanding of the behavior
of other animals or humans." According to his theory, "this
ability resulted from the capacity of one animal to detect (via
its nervous system), analyze, and synthesize signal-stimuli
given off by another animal."

Kazhinskiy further theorized, "the signals were transmit-
ted in the form of a 'bioradiational sight ray' and were ana-
lyzed by the percipient animal as a result of its Pavlovian conditioning." This "reflex understanding" would be a form of
perception which would lie outside the five senses as we know
them, but would have a bio-energetic and not a metaphysical
explanation. As such, it would meet the requirements of the
flesh-and-blood advocates of Bigfoot research and could be
the subject of scientific investigation and experimental verifi-
cation, and not merely philosophical speculation.

Redfern and Roberts further report that some Soviet
and Czech parapsychologists still use the term "bioradiational rays" to refer to "focusing and concentration of

biological energy by the brain and the optical neural channels." This process of focusing and concentration sounds precisely like what Bigfoot might be using as part of its camouflaging technique. The communication via these rays theoretically provides a direct mind-to-mind link and bypasses the ordinary modes of perception.

If Kazhinskiy's research is valid, the authors note, "then it offers the possibility that the entire animal kingdom of our planet may somehow have the ability to utilize highly advanced mental tools that, largely, elude human beings."

Classified research by the Soviets and Czechs in parapsychology during the 1970s was devoted to investigating the source of such biological energy, its interactions with external fields, and the effects of externally generated fields on animals. The Soviets felt they were making significant advances toward identifying the electromagnetic radiation (EMR) source of biological energy during that period. One Soviet scientist, A. S. Presman, "felt that biological energy and information exchange between living organisms was the result of electromagnetic field (EMF) interactions between individuals or between the individual and the environment."

Presman's research revealed what he believed was widespread telepathic ability among animals and speculated on the lack of such abilities in humans. He believed, similar to what Sheldrake concluded about telepathy, that, "electromagnetic signaling is universal between animals, but not between humans who may have lost the capability for such communication as a result of evolution and the development of verbal and artificial communication channels." He did feel it was possible for occasional cases of "spontaneous telepathy" among humans, but considered it to be rare and atavistic. He considered man as the "least suitable animal for studying telepathy or what he called "electromagnetic communication."

Although we can extrapolate how this cited European research in telepathy among animals might apply to the supposed mental powers of mystery hominids, Sheldrake's and the Russians' respective research efforts were obviously not specifically related to Bigfoot. However, considerable research also has been done in Russia that *is* specifically related to Bigfoot. Moreover, mainstream science in Russia is much more open to the evidence for the existence of Bigfoot-type creatures and also to the question of their possible psychic powers than their colleagues in the United States.

After years of studying what she called a "relict hominoid" and organizing a dozen expeditions to remote mountains and forests, Maya Bykova, one of the leading Russian authorities on Bigfoot, or Almas as they are called in that country, came to some interesting conclusions. Her fieldwork included documentation of the animal's ability to appear and disappear suddenly, as if dissolving into thin air.

This same ability was documented by American researchers Ann Slate and Alan Berry in their classic book, *Bigfoot*. While acknowledging it is a far-out theory, they wrote of, "ancient Indian legends and other unorthodox events," during their own field research which, "led researchers to suspect that the mind of the Bigfoot might indeed possess this telepathic-hypnotic capability."

They cite a number of cases around the country that suggest, "…the Bigfoot creatures can make themselves invisible, through mind control or delusion of others." Of their own research they write, "There were times when it almost seemed as if the creatures could make themselves invisible, and disappear in a split second. It wasn't a thought that any of the men warmed to or liked to discuss, yet, inexorably, it would surface: were there spiritual or unknown forces at play?"

Tom has personally witnessed Bigfoot's disappearing act. It was comforting for him to find out other investigators had witnessed or documented it, or he would have seriously doubted his own sanity. As it is, he has been challenged to understand this strange phenomenon:

> In my past experiences, even at times when I could
> tell they were close to me, I would approach them
> and they would throw their voices, and make
> themselves seem to be invisible to the human
> eye. No matter how positive the situation was, by
> the vibrations I was feeling at the moment, they
> would let me know they wanted me to get only
> so close. At times when I was going to take them
> gifts, food mostly, they would appear in front of
> me for a second and seem to walk through a door

in nature, where they would just simply disappear, as if they were showing me their mastery of nature and physics as well. Physics mostly deals with natural phenomena like sound, force, electricity, lights in nature, and they certainly seem to have that domain of the natural environment under their control in ways humans do not. Until mainstream science figures out that there are certain elements in nature we clearly do not understand, like the theory of multi-universes, for example, we will get nowhere in understanding the nature of these beasts.

Bykova rejected supernatural explanations for this ability and favored instead the idea that mystery hominids possess an unexplained defense mechanism that makes them "invisible" to humans. She explained this ability by saying the creature "camouflages its biofield." She thought this was a case of "psychological suggestion" directed inward by the creature on itself, not outward. This idea was also proposed by her colleague, Professor Porshnev, who further postulated that excessive psychic, nervous, or physical strain triggers spontaneous natural "autotraining" that leads to a profound lethargic state in which all brain activity ceases. He theorized this does not produce complete physical disappearance, but does produce virtual invisibility in respect to would-be observers.

The idea is the creature "plays possum" by stopping the activity of its brain, and dissolves into its surroundings as an extension of its other camouflaging abilities. This sounds like how the ancient Apache scouts were said to hide in the blind spots of their enemies or intended prey.

The Paranormal vs. Flesh-and-Blood Research Schism

Peculiar circumstances surrounding Bigfoot sightings have led to the notion the creatures are not physically real animals. The fact they often seem to vanish without a trace, as we have discussed, sometimes eluding extensive organized hunts after having been seen in a given area for a short time, on the surface supports the idea that Bigfoot are not only psychic, but maybe entirely paranormal. This situation has led to a schism among Bigfoot researchers and research organizations who have split into the so-called "paranormal" and "flesh-and-blood" camps.

Advocates of the paranormal explanation of Bigfoot express opinions ranging all the way from claiming the creatures are no more than phantoms to thinking of them as demon shapeshifters or interdimensional travelers. The flesh-and-blooders dismiss all these views as utter nonsense. They point to physical evidence, especially footprints, many of which have been authenticated by objective experts like Chester Moore and Jeff Meldrum, to support their stance that Bigfoot is just an undiscovered, although peculiarly elusive, species of ape.

Those who hold this position fear an admission of any sort of paranormal aspect being involved with Bigfoot sightings reduces the entire subject to some kind of New Age, airy-fairy belief system and puts off any serious consideration by mainstream scientific study. This notion is not without merit, but it is not confirmation of a Holy Cow belief system that the two of us are seeking. We are not appealing to religious-type faith or rank mysticism, but by the same token, we believe we should not let whatever our belief system is stand in the way of objective analysis of all relevant data.

In fact, at one time both of us leaned toward our own respective variations of the paranormal theory. It was clear to us the creatures at times are capable of assuming physical form, but it seemed like their ability to do so is limited, framed perhaps by unknown energy conditions. We considered it entirely possible Bigfoot is essentially a being whose source and nature is more metaphysical than physical; a spirit being, as many Native American traditions would say, with psychic powers.

Along with the problem of detection, this strange energy connection and Bigfoot's seeming to have psychic powers has led some writers and researchers to conclude in varying degrees that Bigfoot sightings are essentially paranormal manifestations—psychic events similar to dreams—and do not involve physically real animals. The late John Keel, as described in *The Complete Guide to Mysterious Beings*, thought the creatures are transmogrifications of the energy itself. In *Spirit of Place*, Dr. James Swann explains why he thinks the animals are spirit beings that sometimes manifest into this reality in the form of what he calls "waking visions." Colin and Janet Bord in *Alien Animals* refer to Bigfoot as being among the menagerie of what they call the "alien animals," which sometimes frequent our planet.

Bigfoot encounters, however, are not limited to sporadic window-peeking forays into small towns or isolated houses on the edge of the woods. There is more to Bigfoot than confrontations with startled motorists on lonely country roads or lovers' lanes. It might be reasonable to think these kinds of sightings were somehow intended only for the witnesses involved. But the fact is Bigfoot evidence covers a broad range of what would seem to be the normal day-to-day survival activities of a large primate.

Suspect tracks have been found in isolated areas seldom visited by humans. Weird hairy creatures coming forth from their mysterious lairs to pester humans might be suspected of being hoaxes or paranormal encounters, but in these cases humans have apparently ventured into Bigfoot's territory. Huge, human-like, barefoot tracks have been found among groves of wild plum and hawthorn trees in East Texas, for instance, where there is evidence the creatures were foraging for food. There are similar accounts of such footprints having been found in the deep woods among the gutted remains of deer and feral hogs whose internal organs had been removed and whose intestines had been pulled out and laid alongside the carcasses. Judging from their broken hind legs and their bashed-in skulls, they were apparently killed by being slammed against trees. There is no known animal that kills its prey in this way, and what normal human would be big or strong enough to thus dispatch a two-hundred-pound hog? This emphatically does not seem like the work of a phantom.

All this evidence is enough to convince us Bigfoot is a physical animal and not a non-physical paranormal chimera. But if we are to be thorough in this inquiry, we cannot dismiss the observations of researchers like Keel, Swann, and Bord. The animals are, indeed, frequently seen immediately after the appearance of mysterious lights, and as has been shown, they are definitely sometimes associated with equally mysterious blackouts and power outages, especially of vehicles. What confuses the issue is similar light and energy phenomena are also frequently associated with paranormal phenomena, such as classic haunting cases. The difference is that in the case of Bigfoot encounters, physical evidence is sometimes left, whereas in paranormal events it is not.

Too often when the creatures are said to have psychic powers, they are thereby defined not only as unknown, but as unknowable. As we have seen from the above discussion of psychic research by European scientists, the mystery hairy hominids' mental and sensory abilities might be every bit as strange as those attributed to them by paranormal advocates. As we have also seen, however, we need not appeal solely to metaphysics to account for them.

....

It is precisely this question that is the pivotal point where the nonproductive schism of physical versus paranormal in Western Bigfoot research has historically occurred. The flesh-and-blood advocates must be given their due, however. Too often, advocates of paranormal Bigfoot seek to deify the creatures and set them up as the equivalent of the all-knowing, benevolent UFO Space Brothers who have come to save humanity. We are subjected to unsubstantiated claims of bedroom visitations of materializing Bigfoot, and claims of personal psychic connections to Bigfoot with science-fiction sounding names. It is not our intention to open that can of worms.

Even short of this extreme, paranormal models of explanation are frequently too quick to throw out the physical evidence and to abandon objectivity. Half-baked theories of shapeshifting and interdimensional travel are set forth with no basis in actual observation and are not experimentally verifiable. At that point, investigation and research end and speculation and belief take over.

So, in this sense the flesh-and-blooders are correct. Speculation about the creatures' alleged psychic abilities does tend to belittle the legitimacy of Bigfoot research to established science and deservedly so. But is this necessarily the case? Perhaps this situation is as much due to the limitations of the research approach of Western science as it is to the inadequacy of the paranormal models.

Our views should not be construed as an attempt to redefine the Bigfoot phenomenon in ways that keep it a mystery and something we will never be able to know—far from it. That gets us nowhere and just puts us right back into the arena of opinion and belief. We insist, also, that we have not in effect made up a mythical beast and then resorted to these exotic arguments to defend our cherished beliefs. What motivated both of us from the beginning was that we came across various phenomena in our experience for which we could find no recognized scientific explanation.

Chester Moore once said he thinks most of the so-called Bigfoot experts don't want the mystery to ever be solved, lest the inadequacies of their own theories be exposed. Until then, they can keep writing books with their expert opinions. We agree, there are no Bigfoot experts, because none of us know for sure what we're dealing with. But we think the evidence presented here suggests Bigfoot are *both* flesh-and-blood *and* paranormal beings. They are physically real animals with astounding psychic powers. This conclusion supports an exciting approach to future research that would recognize both the physical and paranormal parameters of Bigfoot sightings and would be in denial of neither.

If there are electromagnetic effects associated with Bigfoot sightings and their psychic abilities, as Sheldrake and the Russian research suggest, then these would leave a trail just as surely as do footprints. Electromagnetism can be measured and quantified, and although it is difficult to say what it might look like, we should be able to develop new or utilize existing instrumentation to follow such a trail.

EIGHT

Wild, Hairy Hominids, Mystery Light-Forms, and Anomalous Energy Fields

The Ghost Light Phenomenon

From scores of eyewitness interviews and from our personal experiences gained through decades of field research, we are led to conclude the wild, hairy man/beasts in their natural environment are likely to be finely attuned to something like the bioradiational energy rays postulated by the Czech and Russian scientists mentioned in the previous section. Theoretically, this could impart extraordinary mental abilities on them, which along with other camouflaging techniques, would give them the advantage and make them next to impossible to see or track down in the wild. Bigfoot could be a race of beings that has a profound wisdom of this subtle energy and its relationship to consciousness and perception. They seem to be able to use this knowledge in some form of mind control or hypnosis that not only keeps them hidden from the view of mankind, but possibly could allow them to alter the form of themselves they present for our view.

We further believe this energy can appear in a concentrated or focused form as unidentified mystery lights. Such strange luminosities are present in the area Tom has studied in the form of the Brown Mountain Lights and in Rob's study area as the Bragg Road Light. They are two of the most well-known instances of a scientifically recognized anomaly commonly referred to as the standing ghost light phenomenon, so called because the light-forms have been known to recur in the same highly localized areas within a range of a few miles for decades, or longer.

There is no reliable information about the frequency of the lights' appearances. On any given night, one might go to a ghost light location and see nothing, but over an extended period of time the chance of seeing one of the basketball-sized luminous spheres would increase. The unanimous opinion of international research in the United States, Japan, the United Kingdom, Canada, and Europe, as detailed in Rob's *In the Big Thicket: On the Trail of the Wild Man,* is that the lights represent some little understood aspect of the earth's electromagnetic energy field, possibly related to solar magnetic radiation storms.

Their electromagnetic nature is confirmed by repeated reports of electrical disturbances associated with the lights, such as blackouts of car lights, the stopping of car engines, and radio interference. Such occurrences are commonly reported of the Bragg Road ghost light and are detailed in Rob's first book. What is not so well known, although it was consistently reported by such pioneering mystery primate investigators as Keel, Persinger, Swan, Slate, and Berry, is that such disturbances are also frequently associated with mystery hominids. This association is virtually ignored by current organized research groups, but it strongly implies that ghost lights and Bigfoot are causally related, especially since these two anomalous phenomena typically recur with a periodicity of an unknown but regular cycle in the same very specific locations.

Independent of Rob's investigations in this regard, Tom's research findings led him to believe the creatures he was encountering on his property were somehow related to weird light-forms that started showing up in the photos he was getting as early as a decade ago, and specifically to the Brown Mountain Lights, as detailed in his field notes below:

My cameras are picking up weird, bizarre life forms or some type of energy that I am not familiar with nor have I ever seen before.

Out of sixty-some odd photos, only one was interesting. It was almost a cloud of light or fog moving through the picture area.

Again, I am getting photographs of beautiful, round luminous lights. They appear almost cellular in nature and they were taken at night. To me this is not logical. There appears to be some uniformity to them at times, and then the next time they appear to be relaxed or spread out.

Some of the photos I take with my trail cams now come back blank. I can't understand it, it's like the film has been exposed by something, but there's nothing showing up in the frame. I do have some photographs of lights moving, round glowing objects in the woods, mostly at night or in the mornings.

Many times my machine takes pictures and I am unable to see anything in them. Most of this activity appears to be at night. But this time I got some good ones. One such photo is truly a mystery—a bright light, and behind it two boxlike probes or trails. What it is, is puzzling. I've never seen or photographed anything like it before. It looks like a life form, but it may not be known to man, biology, or even science fiction as we know it. I feel indeed honored to be lucky enough to have such photos. The next frame shows gas-like vapors or a mist. What this is, again, is another piece to the puzzle.

Yesterday I called Gander Mountain Supply Company where we bought the game trail camera, and told them I was getting exposures that seemed to be of apparently nothing. The man I spoke with tried to assure me this was impossible. There had to be something there, he said, to trip the camera. Maybe it was something small, animals you can't see.

I told the man I saw white, almost electric, shapes moving in and out of the foliage about eight hundred yards up the mountain. I watched for about thirty minutes to make sure my eyes weren't playing a trick on me. I was for sure seeing something, but what I do not know.

Last night again I looked on the mountain to see if I might be able to see the white shapes again. I saw them. I know for sure now what I saw was real, but what it is, is still unknown.

The mysterious lights also keep reappearing. I haven't yet figured out what they are. However, I do live close to the area and gorge where the Brown Mountain Lights go. Maybe this is what I have behind my property.

At first, all I was after was an elusive ape that exists in folklore and also in peoples' minds. Variable A is: I've got that "proof" with the photographs. For the time being, I know there is something there. For now I will leave it at that.

Variable B is: I've got photos of a series of lights that are mobile, they have shape and form and they are capable of triggering the infrared beam that is connected to my camera in the study area.

These lights also move in groups, and some seem to have uniformity in their movement. They also travel in the day as well as night, but activity seems to be more in the evenings. Some photos show they are relaxed, sometimes they appeared very uniform in size, very rigid structures with shape and definition. They do appear to have a purpose, but that purpose is a mystery. I want to find out more about them. I wonder if variables A and B are connected. What is the link between these mysterious lights and the ape-man? At this point I don't know, but it certainly makes things a little more fascinating.

In my simple mind I am not after UFOs or mysterious lights moving through the woods, which are showing up on my game cam photos and are also a puzzle. All I want is the ape-man, the Bigfoot. No wonder no one's ever captured him—maybe that's his UFO. Maybe he can actually transform his body from matter to a cloud-like vapor that becomes energy and light and then re-materializes in solid form at will. This sounds like science fiction, and I don' believe it for a minute, but I do have three mysterious variables I am dealing with when I am only after one.

One mystery has led to another, and at least I won't get bored for the time being. I will still concentrate my energy on solid forms, something that breathes, eats, and sleeps. To me I know it's here. It has a body and leaves physical evidence where it travels from one point to another. UFOs and moving lights don't. However, the lights do make my infrared monitor react and make photographs. The lights could be a type of electromagnetic current coming through the earth's surface. At this point, I am not sure. Maybe the future holds answers to some of these mysterious phenomena. I hope so!

Not only are there long-term established histories of Bigfoot-type creature sightings near the Big Thicket and Brown Mountain ghost light locations, but a brief survey of the available literature will show the Yakima Indian Reservation lights in Washington, the Gonzales Light in Louisiana, the Gurdon Light in Arkansas, and the Hornet Spook Light location in Missouri, to name a few, also have histories of numerous and repeated sightings of mysterious hairy primates nearby to where the lights recur.

To summarize the case for there being an electromagnetic parameter to the mystery of Bigfoot's appearances and its elusiveness, and to demonstrate that this is not some harebrained theory based on specious or anecdotal information, consider this passage from his classic book, *The Complete Guide to Mysterious Beings*, by John A. Keel:

Lost Gap, a heavily wooded area about five miles east of Meridian, Mississippi, was gripped with "monster mania" in 1962. It began when a group of teenagers reported seeing a green-eyed monster six to nine feet tall. Soon there were dozens of other corroborating witnesses. Chief Deputy Alton Allen said he was convinced the monster existed, and a huge search party was organized. Bloodhounds and a helicopter were brought into play, but nothing was found. Nine years earlier, according to one story, railroad men working the area where the monster was later seen found that their compasses would not work.

A compass malfunctioning is a dead giveaway there are electromagnetic forces at play, and again we see the association with the creatures. A few years ago while doing field research in the Big Thicket, Rob and a friend from Austin experienced just such a case of a compass not working properly under mysterious circumstances. At the time, he didn't associate it with Bigfoot or the wild man, but evidence collected since then convinces us it was connected to the creatures. The compass malfunction was part of a more encompassing phenomenon we call the "eerie silence." We have also had this strange and unexpected phenomenon described to us by others who have been subjected to it.

When the eerie silence dawns, it may be like the dead canary in a coal mine and serve as a warning that the creatures are nearby employing their mental projection of magnetic energy. Whatever causes cars to stall and their electrical systems to black out when Bigfoot are around might also short-circuit nervous systems or induce dormancy and helplessness in their intended prey in the wild. When human beings are subjected to this weird effect, it has mystifying and sometimes terrifying results.

The following is Rob's account of how he came to recognize this uncanny phenomenon.

The Eerie Silence

Some ancient cultures, particularly among the native peoples of the Americas and Celtic Europe, seemed to have been attuned to the mysteries of strange lights and subtle energies. They were very concerned about identifying places where these energy fields were said to periodically focus and attached great importance to the astrological significance of the equinoxes and solstices in predicting when the focusing effect would occur. Some scholars think such cultures believed the times and places this occurred provided temporary openings between this world and other realities.

Curiously, for reasons which remain essentially unknown, they also built long, perfectly straight roads or lines, sometimes called ley lines, connecting these places to their cultural and ceremonial centers. Their belief seemed to have been that somehow the lines or roads acted as a kind of conduit for distributing the subtle energy from the focal points to the rest of their countries. A full discussion of this is beyond the scope of this work. Suffice it to say, the absolute straightness of the lines was universally considered by those cultures which concerned themselves with building them to be essential. Since Bragg Road is an eight-mile long, almost perfectly straight line, I had often wondered if its straightness had somehow attracted energy from other points in the Big Thicket, thereby producing the famous ghost lights.

With this in mind, my friend Stan Shaw and I decided to make a spur-of-the-moment trip to Bragg Road for the spring equinox of 1995. We thought it would be interesting to be on the Ghost Road at the precise instant when the equinox occurred. Stan calculated the exact time would be 2:32 a.m. The four-and-a-half- hour drive from Austin worked out perfectly. We arrived at Bragg Road a little after 2:00 a.m.

About an hour after our arrival, during lulls in our conversation, it dawned on me something peculiar was happening. I asked Stan to stop talking for a while and listen. He replied he couldn't hear anything unusual, in fact, the woods were very quiet. That was what was so weird. The woods were quiet, all right—way too quiet.

For miles in every direction, we were surrounded by a vast network of woods and swamplands populated by untold millions of insects and frogs. The nighttime cacophony of these noise-makers is an unpleasant and inescapable fact of life in the Big Thicket. This is not even to mention sometimes noisy nocturnal animals, such as coyotes or owls. Yet, while we listened in amazement, not a single creature was making even the slightest sound of any kind. I am a veteran of many overnight outings in those woods, and I had never experienced such a thing. All around us, it was as stone dead silent as a tomb. Even the normally ever-present sound of breezes flowing through the treetops was absent.

Out of curiosity and for future research purposes, before we arrived we had decided to determine how close the straight-line road aligns with magnetic north. We checked Stan's compass and watched as the needle bobbed several times and then began to spin slowly. We watched in amazement for several minutes, expecting the needle to come to a rest and point to magnetic north, but the needle never stopped spinning. There had to be very unusual magnetic conditions at play for a compass to malfunction in such a way.

Were these same magnetic conditions also affecting the insects, birds, reptiles, and mammals, inducing some kind of temporary stupor and producing the utter silence that enveloped us? It didn't take long before the creepy atmosphere got on our nerves. It was compounded by the spooky feeling that we were being watched. Judging from what I was to learn later about the circumstances surrounding this phenomenon of a sudden eerie silence, the wild man might well have been watching us.

Not long after the release of my first book, *In the Big Thicket: On the Trail of the Wild Man,* friends and family held a book signing for me in Sour Lake. A good many people showed up, including a surprise visit by Rand Trusty and Jerry Hestand, two members of the Texas Bigfoot Research Center. This was the first I had heard of their group, which has since changed its name to the Texas Bigfoot Research Conservancy, but I was delighted to know that others were claiming there are unknown hairy hominids in East Texas and investigating sightings.

They were sufficiently impressed by the evidence presented in my book and by the vast expanse of lush vegetation they had seen on the way to Sour Lake, to believe Hardin County held plenty of suitable habitat for the ape-like creatures. They had been investigating sightings in East Texas in similar environments for several years. They were not, however, sympathetic to my claim that there was a connection between the sightings of such creatures and the ghost light phenomenon. In fact, they seemed doubtful the ghost lights were a real phenomenon at all, and not just the product of local folklore and imagination.

I assured them I was not making up the fact that there had been a number of Big Thicket wild man sightings actually on Bragg Road itself, where the ghost light is seen. There were even those who said they saw the light immediately before the mysterious hairy creature showed up. One couple told me that they were horrified to see the light and the creature simultaneously. They were right to be unnerved, as this indicates the presence of multiple creatures that at times travel in pairs or groups.

Like many serious Bigfoot investigators, they thought such accounts detract from the legitimacy of unknown hominid sightings—that introducing things like ghost lights could reduce Bigfoot to the realm of the paranormal. Still, they were curious enough to accept my invitation to escort them to the Ghost Road where they could at least assess its environs as potential Bigfoot habitat. Without their saying so, I was sure they never expected to see any mysterious lights.

We drove about two or three miles up the Ghost Road from the south end. About fifteen minutes later, we were all surprised to see a half dozen or so lights moving about and blinking in the tree branches fifteen or twenty feet off the ground just behind us and to our right as we faced northward. Rand was the first to spot them, and he was very excited. Eight of us were there, and we all saw the lights. They were about the size of golf balls, however, compared to only one basketball-size light in the more typical ghost light sighting. They remained in the tree branches and did not hover over the roadbed to allow us a better look. After several minutes of almost seeming to play hide-and-seek with us, the lights simply vanished.

My Bigfoot investigator visitors were dramatically converted by their experience, and all admitted there must be something to the ghost light stories after all. I explained to them my theory that wild man appearances may somehow be related to the same unknown energy sources that produce the ghost lights. I went on to tell them stories of other encounters with strange energy manifestations I have experienced over the years on the Ghost Road and in nearby parts of the Big Thicket. I mentioned the time Stan and I were spooked out by the eerie silence, the spinning compass needle, and the feeling of being watched.

This last story seemed to strike a familiar chord with Jerry and Rand. They told me they had a similar experience during a Bigfoot investigation stakeout near Caddo Lake in northeast Texas. The group sent a team there to try to obtain recordings of the creatures' vocalizations, which had been recently been reported in that area. Sure enough, in the late-night hours after midnight, they heard the spine-tingling, ungodly loud howls. Then they experienced something totally unexpected and were totally unprepared for—complete and utter silence. Like Stan and I did, they found the tomb-like quiet to be unnerving. After hearing the loud howling, the sudden silence affects the mind strangely. Your imagination can run wild as you feel are being watched and wonder if the beast is creeping up on you in the silence.

My guests still saw no connection between their experience and mine and Stan's, but because of the compass malfunction, I knew the silence on the Ghost Road had a bizarre energy component. I wondered whether this was not just a coincidence, but rather that their experience was a case of the same kind of energy being manifested with an appearance of one of the mysterious creatures. Within a few weeks, my suspicions were confirmed, and I was to learn of several other such incidences.

I had a meeting with the promotions manager of a major book store in Austin about doing a book signing there. It turns out she was a native East Texan. Without my mentioning anything about the eerie silence phenomenon, she began to tell me of a frightening experience some friends of hers from back home had recently had on a camping trip. She didn't know exactly where they were, but it was in one of the national forests in East Texas. Her friends had already retired for the night and were in sleeping bags in their tent. They heard what sounded like several large animals approaching them, and then the normal night sounds of the woods lapsed into complete and utter silence. As they cowered in the fetal position, they could see the shadows of several huge, hulking forms walk past them, cast by the moonlight on the walls of their tent. She said her friends were absolutely traumatized by their experience.

A short time later, I was doing a radio talk show in Beaumont. A caller told me of his experience while squirrel hunting in Jasper County. Dusk was approaching when he heard an unfamiliar howling sound that he could not identify as coming from any animal he knew. Then the woods went completely silent. Unnerved, he decided to leave the woods before darkness fell. As he made his retreat, the woods remained unnaturally quiet, except for the muffled sounds of footsteps from something massive and heavy that seemed to be following him.

The caller identified himself as an experienced hunter who, as he said, "wasn't afraid of anything." But he admitted that he was so scared the hair literally stood up on the back of his neck. What spooked him the most, he said, was how quiet it was. He ended his call by saying he would never hunt in those woods again.

Not long after that, I attended a cryptozoology conference hosted by Chester Moore. One of the presenters, Jim Lansdale, played a video of a Bigfoot hunter who had a rare sighting in north Louisiana of four of the animals, what appeared to be two adults and two juveniles. From his secluded vantage point, he observed them for some time. At the end of his interview, almost as an afterthought, he mentioned something peculiar that had happened during his sighting. He said right after the apes appeared everything in the woods went spookily and disturbingly quiet, such as he had never experienced before.

I talked to Chester about this strange phenomenon, which seems to occur in at least some Bigfoot sightings. Chester admitted he and some of his friends have experienced something similar during one of their nocturnal hunts on a bayou in Orange County near the Texas/Louisiana state line. He said everything around them went dead quiet, just as I had described. What seemed even more peculiar was he could hear typical nighttime woods noises very faintly further down the bayou, but right where he and his party were, there stirred not the slightest sound. Even though they were packing considerable firepower Chester said they felt uneasy and decided to abandon the hunt.

It's clear in each of these separate accounts that the sudden eerie silence had a disturbing impact on those who experienced it. In each case, the silence was mentioned as somewhat of an oddity without any awareness or knowledge by the witnesses of others having experienced anything similar in their own encounters. These cases show enough of a pattern that the eerie silence phenomenon should be taken as a corollary of at least some Bigfoot encounters. As the spinning compass Stan and I witnessed indicates, it should also be taken as an indication that anomalous or aberrant energy fields were at play.

Episodes of the eerie silence could be instances of the creatures' employing their camouflaging ability—in some cases for stalking game and in others for eluding detection by humans—by the mind-to-mind mental projection of a type of bio-electromagnetic energy in a manner suggested by the Russian research we have considered. The projected energy could have a numbing effect on the nervous systems of other life forms, temporarily stunning them into silence and making the Bigfoot invisible to them. We should also consider the likelihood suggested that the energy in question is the same kind, if not the identical energy, which produces mystery light-forms.

If the "eerie silence" phenomenon is in fact a result of Bigfoot employing some kind of energy field projection, it should have an EM signature, which is something that can be measured and quantified. Bigfoot may not only leave behind a trail of footprints, it might leave behind an energy trail as well. If Bigfoot uses this energy in stalking its prey, perhaps the energy can also be used to stalk Bigfoot.

The Luminous Energy Stream

About six years after Stan and I experienced the eerie silence, I made yet another unplanned trip with a friend to my old Big Thicket stomping grounds. What we witnessed provides intriguing clues into the nature and source of the energies associated with mystery lights and unknown wild hominids, as well as how they affect the mind.

Farrell Brenner is a now retired health care professional whose former practice in Austin specialized in the effects— both positive and negative—of ambient environmental energies. He also happens to have been a longtime friend of mine who about a year before had successfully treated me for uncharacteristic symptoms of psychological depression a few months after I had returned home from an encounter with mysterious energy fields in the Big Thicket.

Late one spring afternoon, we had a casual conversation about the health benefits of exposure to negative ions while hiking on his and his partner Alice's property in the Hill Country a few miles west of the city. Farrell explained that waterfalls, which are abundant in those hills, are one of nature's best ways of producing negative ions, and that generally the more negative ions you are exposed to, the better and more uplifted you feel. Since many diseases, such as high blood pressure and cardiovascular problems are directly or indirectly associated with stress, he said, the potential of negative ion therapy is huge.

The calming effect of negative ions produced by moving water was just one reason it is so relaxing to hang out by a waterfall or by crashing waves at the seaside or to spend time in the deep woods, which also has that effect.

Our modern cities are increasingly more toxic, he further explained. This is not just from air and water pollution, which you would expect, but also from energy pollution. We live within an energy maze otherwise known as the utility grid. Power lines are everywhere and virtually every home and office is wired to the max for everything from cable TV to wireless internet. Most people these days work in front of a computer screen forty plus hours a week and then go home and spend another two or three hours a day in front of a TV screen, playing video games, or surfing the internet. All of this leads to overexposure to positive ions. And that causes health problems. Prolonged exposure to positive ions or not enough exposure to negative ions can interfere with the body's production of serotonin, and that can lead to difficulty sleeping, headaches, irritability, heart palpitations, depression, and extreme fatigue. It all adds up to a vicious cycle. Understanding how to utilize negative ions and how to avoid or protect ourselves from the influence of positive ions can help us break that cycle.

I questioned him about the energy I confronted in the Thicket and why it seemed to have had such a negative impact on me. Since it was a naturally occurring field, why was it so detrimental? He explained that in nature, energies are subject to positive and negative polarity. If there was an energy source that made me sick, it was probably producing positive ions, but there very likely could also be a focal point of negative ions somewhere nearby in those woods.

I had a hunch I knew where it was and that it was not far from the place I had seen all the tiny red pinpoint lights on a prior trip that Farrell thought had been the source of my problem. My gut told me the focal point might be further south down the bayou, and that it could be the actual source of the famous ghost light on Bragg Road.

Farrell admitted my stories were making him curious. Since it was Friday and neither of us had anything planned for the weekend, before you knew it, we were on the road making the five-hour drive to the east. At around two in the morning we reached our destination, a trailhead in the Lance Rosier Unit of the Big Thicket National Preserve near Saratoga.

The next morning we hiked to the west bank of the cypress-lined Little Pine Island Bayou and followed it downstream for a couple of miles to where it intersects a pipeline right-of-way. We sat a while to rest on a log. I had just told Farrell to keep his eyes open because there had been a number of wild man sightings along such pipelines due to the long range of uninterrupted views through dense woods they provide, when I happened to notice something strange about fifty yards north of us, up the pipeline along the ridge of a slight rise. There was a visible energy field shimmering across the cleared open space.

At first we thought it might be similar to the mirage effect produced by sunlight shining through heat waves radiating off the pavement of a highway, which from a distance looks like water. However, it wasn't hot that day, and there was no pavement. Moreover, when we got up and walked toward the shimmering energy field, it did not recede from us like a mirage would. Instead, it got closer and closer until with no hesitation we were able to actually step into it.

It was no more difficult to see the sparkling light close up than it was from a distance, and we both experienced the perspective of actually standing within the field. We both also could discern and agree upon its dimensions, which remained clearly visible. It flowed like a small stream with very discrete boundaries about ten paces wide and twenty feet high through the dense woods. I asked Farrell if maybe the pipeline was producing ions by having crude oil flowing through it, trying to figure out what could cause such an anomaly.

He pointed out that the field was flowing almost perpendicular to the pipeline. If it was somehow being produced by the pipeline, it would run along it or parallel to it. What we are able to see might have been the play of sunlight on the energy field rather than the energy itself. So, in that way at least it actually would be similar to sunlight reflecting off heat waves and explain why we couldn't see it extending on either side of the pipeline into the woods.

After spending about ten minutes bathing in the glittering flow and reveling in the uplifting effect of negative ions, Farrell suggested we move on and not overdo it until we knew more about its source and the nature of what we were dealing with. I agreed and recommended heading back north on the pipeline right-of-way and see if it would be an easier route back to the trailhead and the truck. Since we had found an activated energy manifestation in the area, I was eager to see what might be taking place on the Ghost Road and whether any lights might be visible there in daylight. We had gone no more than about a hundred yards when we turned back and looked.

It amazed us that the glowing energy field was so visible in broad daylight. Viewed from that distance, it glistened and sparkled in a way reminiscent of the play of sunlight on running water or of bright light shining through the side of a huge glass aquarium. Unfortunately, neither of us had thought to bring a camera with us to document such an astonishing sight.

After we had covered about two miles following the clear path the pipeline provided, a marked trail through dense woods opened up on our left. Sure enough, it led us directly back to the main trailhead and Farrell's truck. I told Farrell I was coming back as soon as I could, and enthusiastically made mental notes of landmarks along the trail. He pointed out there seems to be a periodicity of fluctuations of these things that could be linked with a number of variables. The energy was not likely to be active in the same place all the time, and I should not be surprised if it was absent when I came back.

That made sense because the ghost light on Bragg Road is not always visible, and as far as I knew, no one can predict when it will be. But I wondered what the variables are. Farrell's response was more research needed to be done, but basically the variables could involve phases of the moon or sunspot activity, and there could also be a natural rhythmic flow of energy in what some speculate is a planetary grid on the earth's surface. Or all of these factors are involved.

I knew about the Becker-Hagens planetary grid model and had strongly suspected there could be something to it. In my first book, I had already documented the fact that electromagnetic anomalies are not confined to the ghost lights on Bragg Road in the Big Thicket region. In fact, on that particular grid map, eight grid lines appear to converge somewhere in the Thicket. That point could be what we were looking for. These convergent lines include the line corresponding with the 30 degrees north parallel, along which documented anomalous light phenomena occur all around the world in Mexico, Texas, Louisiana, Florida, the Bermuda Triangle, Egypt, India, and Japan.

Within thirty minutes of climbing back into Farrell's truck, we were at the south entrance of Bragg Road, or Ghost Road as it is popularly known. I had visited this place many times over the years, and although I had actually seen one or more of the lights for which the road is famous on only a few separate occasions, I had learned to expect the unexpected.

The narrow, unpaved, sandy road is lined with thick woods forming a canopy over it for most of its eight miles. Running alongside the road are deep bar ditches which are usually full of water and teeming with snakes, frogs, and other small aquatic swamp creatures. Only a handful of residences and a couple of hunting camps from one end to the other give any indications of human habitation. Since it was still in the early afternoon and there were no ghost light hunters active, the road was virtually uninhabited. It was a new experience for Farrell, and he seemed duly impressed by the starkness of our surroundings.

Farrell noted there was a virtual absence of any source of man-made electromagnetic disturbances anywhere along the road, which is a rarity these days. I recommended we go up north a couple of miles to get away from what little traffic there was at the road's southern intersection with the paved highway that headed to the tiny town of Rye. Farrell pulled over and stopped at my signal when we reached a wide spot on the road's shoulder. Rather than sit and wait, we decided to drive slowly and continue toward the north end to see if we noticed anything.

It was a good choice. Within maybe a half mile of where we started, we found a smaller stream of energy similar to what we had seen along the pipeline in the woods. It had the same appearance and discrete boundaries, and was flowing in the same general southeast to northwest direction at a slight angle off the perpendicular of the Ghost Road's almost perfect north-south alignment.

Farrell acknowledged I had likely been right about the source of the lights on the Ghost Road actually being elsewhere in the woods and that what we were seeing was probably the cross-section of one of the arms of a spiral-shaped energy field several miles, or maybe tens of miles, in diameter. The center of that spiral could well be the point on the Becker-Hagens map where those eight grid lines cross, he said, but even that point might not be entirely stationary. It could move around some with the earth's rotation and orbit or from other unknown variables.

I had been out there at night before and witnessed some unusual electromagnetic properties, even when there was no light-form visible. One time we were in my cousin's new Suburban and there was a noticeable dimming of its headlights and panel lights when we crossed a particular place on the road. The spot was about the same width of what we were seeing, maybe fifteen to twenty feet. Another time my car battery was completely dead the morning after I spent a few hours on the Ghost Road the night before. That battery was nowhere near needing replacement. It should have lasted at least a good two more years. We never could figure out what could have so completely drained it. I had to buy a new one because we could not get it to hold a charge.

I also knew of reliable reports from people whose vehicles have completely gone dead on Bragg Road. Sometimes car engines have suddenly cut off, the electrical systems shut down, and the lights blacked out, and they would not come back on or re-start for several minutes.

No doubt we were dealing with an immense and unpredictable energy source, the full range and potential effects of which remain a mystery. Anything that could short out a car battery like that could well have a deleterious effect on the human nervous system. It could also be what was somehow being manipulated by the alleged mental powers of the wild man/Bigfoot creatures to likewise temporarily short out or suspend the nervous systems of its prey and pursuers. We agreed the subject needed more study, but despite those sobering considerations, I could not wait to come back to where we saw the glowing energy stream.

In no more than a couple of weeks I did make it back, only this time I was alone.

I turned off the pavement of Highway 770 a few miles east of Saratoga onto a dirt road toward the entrance of the Rosier Park unit of the Preserve. Thoughts of my mom having been born in that town and my grandmother having been a friend of Lance Rosier, the Cajun barber and self-taught naturalist for whom that part of the Big Thicket Preserve was named, drifted through my mind. The old oil field road happened to run by the cemetery where my great-grandfather was buried. It felt appropriate to stop and briefly pay homage to him and my ancestors on both sides of the family who were so linked to this land and its ancient, fabled woods.

His tombstone was near the biggest southern red cedar tree I have ever seen. Its great size dominated the graveyard and reminded me that some ancient peoples like the Celts revered such large trees. They were said to be indicators of places where the mysterious earth energies concentrate. These thoughts and my impending visit to where we saw the radiant stream of energy put me in a somber and reflective mood as I drove the remaining four miles to the trailhead. I rolled down the windows to suck in the refreshing cool air. There was no one to talk with, and I turned off the radio to take in the sounds and the profound silence of the deep woods.

Instinctively, I slowed my car down to a crawl. The play of light and shadows on the front windshield from the sun shining through the trees had a hypnotic effect. It appeared like a screen in front of me with constantly changing forms that riveted my attention. By the time I reached the clearing where the trail begins, my mind was deeply calmed and focused. I quickly found where the trail leads away from the bayou to the pipeline. The two-mile hike from there to where the bayou curves and intersects the pipeline went by so quickly and effortlessly it seemed like a dream in which Time itself was somehow absent.

Nothing was visible from a hundred yards up the cleared right-of-way like there had been when Farrell and I had been there the week before. At first I thought the energy was not activated at all, but when I got to the actual spot where the pipeline descends toward the bayou, I could clearly discern a fainter version of the same glimmering energy field we had witnessed before. I sat down on a large log that had been left from when they cleared the woods for the right-of-way after I checked to make sure there were no snakes nearby. This was a lesson I had learned from the several times I had almost stepped or sat on a cottonmouth or a copperhead over the years.

It was easy to clear my mind to sensitize myself to the energy. The effect of gazing through the windshield on the short drive through the woods had already done that to a considerable extent. Within a short time, I felt myself settling into even deeper levels of physical and mental relaxation. I had the distinct impression of feeling the energy as a slight prickling sensation on the surface of my skin. Beyond that, I could hear the hum or high-frequency buzzing sound that is frequently reported in places known to exhibit anomalous geomagnetic energy. I made an effort to be as alert as possible and began to consciously scan my surroundings for any possible light-form manifestations, or perhaps even a sudden hairy wild man appearance, but I was completely unprepared for what happened next.

What looked like a TV or movie screen appeared maybe two to three feet in front of me. It filled my entire field of vision and produced a sensation similar to the one I had just experienced with the dappling of sunlight and shade on my car's front windshield. At first I thought I might be dreaming—

that the image of the windshield had been burned into my subconscious and had somehow become superimposed on my normal vision—but I was as aware of my surroundings as I had been before I sat down. Then I thought perhaps my mind had drifted off into that weird hypnagogic transitional state between sleep and wakefulness that can produce vivid dreams the mind has a hard time distinguishing from reality.

I made a conscious effort to wake up, and discovered to my astonishment that it didn't matter whether my eyes were open or shut—the screen stayed in place and was plainly visible. What was displayed on the screen, however, was not the amorphous blending of dark and light that was on the windshield, but a variety of very distinct geometric shapes. Spirals, grids, squares, circles, and zigzag lines of luminosity alternately filled the screen and flashed before my view. This amazed me because it meant I was somehow seeing the screen with something other than my eyes, as if some latent organ of perception had been awakened. It made me wonder whether I wasn't also hearing the electrical hum with something other than my ears.

It was tempting to become absorbed in what I was seeing and hearing and just let go, but a sense of alarm enveloped me. I was getting into something totally foreign to my normal experience, and I was alone in a remote place without anyone knowing where I was. At the time, I did not know whether the screen was hallucinatory or some kind of indicator of an alternate level of consciousness. I needed to know more, but had to be grounded before I proceeded with any further experimentation.

This was an unexpected effect of what I was sure had to be the ghost light producing energy. I wondered if it might have something to do with the perceptual mechanism of how Bigfoot could make itself invisible, or conversely, whether it might have something to do with what makes Bigfoot visible to us in the first place. Would this account for its vanishing when the energy conditions would end, and thus so would its visibility? These questions called for some serious research.

For years, I had read what precious little scholarly and scientific literature was available on the ghost light phenomenon to try to understand what was happening on the Ghost Road. Most of the literature I could find was from the United Kingdom. Paul Devereux's books on what are generally called earth energies in Great Britain were the most informative, especially since he mentioned the same American ghost lights I knew about. Because of this, I became very familiar with his work.

He wrote extensively of traditions among the peoples of the British Isles, who frequently associated their ancient sacred sites with places where some kind of mysterious terrestrial magnetism was known to concentrate. In some cases, the energy in question was said to produce earth lights, unusual light-forms—which we call ghost lights or spook lights in North America. This mysterious energy was also said to have a sensitizing effect on those who were exposed to it, making them more subject to psychic influences and extra-sensory perception.

Thus, ancient British shamanic cultures frequently considered such places to be sacred sites where traffic with the spirit world was enhanced, where the two worlds met or overlapped. Exposure to the energy at the sacred sites under the proper conditions and at propitious times had the capacity of assisting shamans and those guided by them to enter into a trance state. This gave them experiential access to the spirit world and contact with entities therein.

It was clear to me that exposure to anomalous energy fields like those which produce ghost lights in the Big Thicket could also have this effect, perhaps temporarily expanding or altogether altering the range of perception. If this is not just a matter of inducing mere hallucinations, however, I had to wonder what an objective mechanism of this expansion of vision would be, and how this might relate to my curious experience on the pipeline where I saw a screen in front of me filled with a flux of luminous geometric shapes.

As fate would have it, no sooner had I consciously become aware of these questions than I came across a relatively new book by Mr. Devereux. *Shamanism and the Mystery Lines,* it turned out, deals in part with the exact issues that perplexed me. Devereux discusses how shamans use such techniques as ritual dance, drumming, chanting, sleep deprivation, the ingestion of hallucinogenic plants, fasting, gazing at crystals or flashing lights, meditation, and the electrical stimulation of the brain cortex by exposure to unusual magnetic conditions at sacred sites—and any combination thereof—to induce an altered level of consciousness or trance state. According to Devereux, a study of archaic rock art reveals much about the ancient world's fascination with trance.

He points out that several art motifs painted on rock walls and in caves presumably used for initiatory purposes are constant and universal among shamanic cultures that use trance to gain access to the spirity world. Prior to the modern age, this was just about everywhere. Thus, cave-art depictions of humans, animals, and human-animals found in France from Paleolithic Europe, ancient Amerindian rock paintings in Texas, and similar rock art in southern Africa, are all accompanied by "a great plethora of dots, grids, zigzags, curves, and lines," which were the very same forms I saw in the Big Thicket. Had I unwittingly been induced into the beginnings of a shamanic trance experience by mental entrainment with the glimmering energy field?

It would seem so, because Devereux went on to cite anthropological sources who concluded that seeing these same geometric forms is the first stage of going into a deeper trance state, and the forms would appear in front of entranced witnesses on a screen like a slide show or a movie. The forms can be thought of as the background of the world of common perception, perceptible only in an altered state of consciousness, and analogous to the dots and lines of a television that are the basis of the images we see on the screen.

These accounts could not have more accurately described my experience on the pipeline. I could scarcely believe what I was reading. That I should come across this material immediately after having had the strange experience made it seem even more mysterious. It was almost as if a hidden hand from some world beyond were withholding this information from me until the precise moment I would be able to appreciate its significance. Was this another example of a Jungian synchronicity like my experiences in the health food store in Austin and in Chester's boat in the middle of the Sabine River, like a manifestation of some other order of reality, or was this a message from the Bigfoot telling me I was on the right track?

Tom's Photos of Mystery Light-Forms

Tom's findings from the same period as those of Rob's above pretty much summarize what both of us have come to conclude about the significance of the connection of the Bigfoot with mysterious light-forms and strange energy fields:

Based on some of the pictures I have, I think some of these creatures will be way stranger than we will ever be able to imagine. I do think some of the pictures are of a paranormal nature, and I do believe some of what I have may be alien species living among us. That's why they prefer forested areas to stay hidden. As alien as they seem, they may have been here since the beginning of time.

Many of these sightings occur near or on forested areas with unusual electromagnetic anomalies— places diffused with energy. Perhaps the creatures use the energy to shift this thing we call life.

From some of the photos I'm getting of these animals that show strange light-forms with them, I am almost convinced some of these animals are connected to parallel worlds, just as I believe the Bigfoot animal might be. Somehow they utilize the special electromagnetic energy in places like here on my land up in the mountains to wormhole out of our dimension into possibly a parallel world similar to our own, which possibly fits the needs of the Bigfoot creatures and other animals and also provides protection.

This would give some logic to some people and creatures being able to move about as light-forms or energy. I have seen the lights move about with my own two eyes. I have also seen the creatures seem to materialize from thin air in front of me, and dematerialize, as well. This can only be control of a separate dimension, different from our own, or perhaps it comes from a superior technology that would make an eyewitness view some type of bizarre magic.

Any superior technology could appear as magic to our less advanced ways. The line between what one perceives to be good and evil is so fine. It's hard to figure out if they are good or bad, but at this point I am beginning to believe they have paranormal powers. My experiences with the wild man or Sasquatch and the mysterious lights I have both seen and photographed are far too bizarre to have been made up.

Tom has obtained several types of mystery light-forms photographed by a game trail motion-sensitive camera on Tom's property in the same location where the purported Bigfoot photo was taken, all of which can be seen on our website. Note that in one photo there is a light seemingly approaching a squirrel on the ground. The light might have been an entity about to prey on the squirrel, which was probably lured by the food Tom left out for bait to attract the hairy mystery creatures.

A fish-shaped orb light was photographed in 1998 in the Big Thicket National Preserve by Rob on two consecutive frames of high-speed 35 mm film near a bridge where there had allegedly been a history of wild man or Bigfoot sightings. Note that the second shot was taken from the opposite side of the bridge from the first shot from a longer distance, and that the orb has moved to the other side of the bayou and maintained both its shape and depth. Although Rob was not conscious of seeing the orb, this could be an example of what old-timers in the Thicket called "haints" or spirits.

NINE

The Shamanic Connections

The Smoke of the World

The fact that wild, hairy hominids actually exist in North America is taken for granted by many tribes of Native Americans and Native Canadians. The same is true of indigenous cultures with shamanic traditions around the world in such countries as Tibet, Siberia, China, Russia, Malaysia, and Australia. All claim to have had more or less continued contact with as yet unidentified ape-like creatures for centuries. For these peoples, the mysterious beings have always been with us, living in the wild places on the fringe of human society, and just outside the sphere of our everyday awareness. For them there is no need to prove Bigfoot is real.

The sasquatch, yeti, yeren, alma, orang pendek, or yowie, as it is variously called, is said by traditional peoples to have astounding mental powers with which it easily eludes detection in its natural habitat for reasons modern people can scarcely comprehend. They might even say many Bigfoot believers don't understand the nature or origin of these Ancient Ones, or why they are so elusive.

Louella Hilburn, a lady from Spokane who identified herself as a member of the Colville Confederated tribe of Washington state, contacted Rob. She claimed her tribe considers the creatures to be from the spirit world. She also told him much of what he said on the radio show she heard him on made her realize some non-Native Americans are beginning to learn we aren't the only intelligent beings in the universe. We are beginning to understand, she said, "that there are spiritual powers which would enable us to communicate with all the universe and all our relations."

A man who identified himself only as a Mississippi Choctaw also contacted Rob. He said his people have known of what he called the hairy forest people and the ghost lights from time immemorial, and it was about time the rest of the world was beginning to learn of them. The Choctaw reservation in Mississippi is pretty much an extension of the same bottomland forests that cover much of East Texas, Louisiana, and Arkansas, and it's possible they deal with Bigfoot who range throughout that entire area. It was significant that he connected the wild man creatures directly with mystery light-forms, and like Louella and most Native Americans, he associated them with what they call the spirit world.

This sounds like a cop-out. If a living Bigfoot or a dead specimen cannot be produced on demand, all it takes is to say they have psychic powers, or they are spirit beings to keep the mystery alive and lay claim to esoteric knowledge. That is how skeptics of Bigfoot's reality view such claims. There is no mysterious ape and no substance to the tales about them. They are quaint superstitions, innocent reminders of simpler times when science had not yet basically explained how the universe works.

Some more liberal academic commentators in philosophy, psychology, or anthropology—if it occurs to them to look at the evidence for Bigfoot at all—might be willing to attribute a relative order of reality to the fabled beasts. They might say something like: "Bigfoot is real to the people who believe in it, but its reality as a spirit being should be taken metaphorically as a myth, not literally as physically existent."

This opinion might sound reasonable, but it leaves some questions unanswered, and it ignores another belief common among Native American cultures. The Bigfoot are said to live in two worlds—both the unseen spirit world and the physical world—and to be able to pass from one realm to the other at will. That gives them special significance to shamanic peoples as the guardians of the gateway to the land of the dead and the ancestors, and as the allies of shamans and those seeking access to that world.

If Bigfoot really have lived in the wild in close proximity to humans for untold ages, it behooves us to listen closely to what people from traditional cultures have to say about them, as these people are perhaps more in touch with both the natural world and the spirit world than is the average modern urbanite. The spirit world as used here is not to be taken as a fairy tale realm or of a symbolic nature only. It is an objective reality that is beyond the normal perceptual range of the average person. For a Native American to say Bigfoot comes from the spirit world and is a spirit being does not mean its existence is metaphorical and not physically real or that it is a phantom.

You might say it is from a reality slightly out of vibrational synch with this reality and hence invisible to us. For indigenous people, this would largely account for Bigfoot's ability to suddenly vanish. It simply adjusts its wavelength, so to speak, by its powers of mental focus and concentration. This may be an extension of the Apache scouts' ability to hide in the blind spots of their enemies and their intended prey. And then there is the matter of its obvious physicality.

Can a mere metaphor chase down and pick up a highly dangerous two-hundred-pound wild hog in the vine-entangled, swampy muck of the Big Thicket by its hind legs and bash its brains out by slamming it up against a tree trunk? Would vicious hunting dogs, which are otherwise fearless of anything in the form of man or beast, tuck tail and run whimpering from something that is only imaginary in the Smoky Mountains? Clearly, something tangible has to be at work here, and there is no animal known to exist in either of these locales or anywhere else on this continent that can account for it.

In light of our prior considerations of the animal telepathy findings of Dr. Sheldrake in England, and the amazing research and observations of Kazhinskiy, Presman, and Bykova in the old Soviet bloc, the beliefs of the native peoples of both this continent and Eurasia should not seem so superstitious to objective analysis. They are more an affirmation that Bigfoot really do exist, and that these wild, hairy, hominid forest-dwellers actually have the psychic powers with which shamanic cultures credit them.

Moreover, these same cultures might have identified the energy medium through which perhaps both Bigfoot's telepathic power and its ability to suddenly disappear operate. The same energy fields that also manifest as ghost lights and other visible light-forms—what these scientists would call morphic fields or bioradiational energy—are well known to native peoples of North America. Another communication Rob received illustrates this fact and corroborates the message from the Mississippi Choctaw, possibly associating the hairy forest people or wild man with a mysterious luminosity.

A man named Cat Thunder from British Columbia who heard Rob interviewed on *Coast to Coast* said his people, called the Kwakiutls, perform an ancient dance in their potlatches, or ceremonial gatherings, that they call the "Wildman of the Woods" dance. They believe through the dance they can tame and communicate with the wild man. He said their wood-carving artists have created images of the hairy creatures with protruding eyebrows for centuries.

On the back cover of Rob's 2001 book, *In the Big Thicket: On the Trail of the Wild Man*, is a photo of what appears to be a smoke formation, or small fog bank surrounding a tree. It was taken by Rob and his friend, Bill Fleming, with high-exposure 35 mm film on Bragg Road in 1996, and is on our website, Bigfootthebigpicture.net.

Technicians at the lab where it was developed told Rob it was obvious the photo was not shot with a flash. Light from a flash reflected from smoke or a fog bank that close and that dense would have whited-out the entire frame. There were also details on the ground behind the fog that must have been illuminated by it, because they would also have been obscured by the glare from a flash. From this, he could only conclude the smoke or fog was self-luminous. The peculiar thing is it was not visible to either Rob or Bill when the photo was taken.

A glowing small fog bank on Bragg Road that *was* visible to the naked eye, however, had been reported to Rob by two different eyewitnesses. One said the fog formation was about ten to twelve feet in diameter and had a denser and brighter center. To his amazement, he said he watched as the glowing, smoky mass suddenly collapsed inward, making the center larger and brighter, and taking the form of a spherical light about two feet in diameter, which is the most commonly observed dimension of the infamous ghost light.

Rob found that particular witness's testimony hard to believe at the time, but the photo did give it some credibility. Perhaps the cloudy light he and Bill photographed was outside the visible light range for the human eye, but was picked up by their camera. Then Brenda Fleming, Bill's wife, pointed out something about the photo, that supported an even more bizarre eyewitness claim and might further link this unusual light-form with the wild man creatures.

An illuminated fog bank or cloud of smoke on Bragg Road on another occasion was reported to Rob by a woman who said she was terrified to see the wild man appear like it was materializing in the fog or stepping out of it. When viewed by turning the image on the book cover a quarter turn clockwise, the fog appears to have the face of a weird, shaggy humanoid creature hidden in it. Step back a couple feet from it, and the depth, distinct facial features, and hairiness are easier to see. In cultures that practice shamanism the faces of spirit beings sometimes appear in the smoke of their ceremonial fires. In this case the entire smoky mass seems to be taking the form of the head of one colossal wild man. The name of the Kwakiutl tribe translates to "Smoke of the World."

Cat Thunder heard Rob talking about the illustration on the book cover and thought there might be a connection between his tribe's name and what Bill and Rob photographed. Is this just a string of coincidences or did the Kwakiutl see the face of the wild man in the smoke of their campfires? Do they have some kind of collective memory of members of their tribe witnessing the wild man emerge from a glowing cloud of smoke, or does it still appear to them? The traditions, and even the name of this tribe, could well indicate another wild man/Bigfoot and weird energy connection.

Safety Concerns

It might well be that the majority of Bigfoot sightings reports are coming only from those who had the blind luck to get away. This could be especially true of those times when the witnesses also experienced the eerie silence. In those cases, the Bigfoot may have already deployed the psychic powers attributed to them by native peoples enough to have stunned the surrounding wildlife. Those witnesses consistently speak of being horrified and of having odd fear reactions, like having the hair on the backs of their necks stick up. Maybe they were fortunate enough to have crossed the path of a Bigfoot who happened to have a full stomach or who did not feel threatened, or who otherwise just happened to have been in a good mood.

The tendency of researchers is to assume the Bigfoot are harmless and loveable, almost like giant teddy bears, or that a rifle of sufficient caliber would provide protection. In light of the above considerations, and for public safety, we should be aware that both of these assumptions might not be true. We really don't know what we are dealing with in the wild, hairy hominids or under what circumstances they might prove to be dangerous and deadly.

As the human population expands into former wildlife habitat, there are increasingly more unfortunate cases of people being attacked by wildlife like bears, cougars, coyotes, and feral hogs. The consequences of meeting up with a Bigfoot are unpredictable and could be devastating. If the growing numbers of researchers continue to ignore the possibility of hairy wild hominids having unusual mental powers, they could potentially be exposed to considerable danger. It is widely believed among Russian peasants, for example, that a face-to-face encounter with an Alma leads the luckless witness to utter madness, and the consequences could be far more severe.

It is a fact not widely publicized, but documented by Steve Paulides, a retired police officer, that people have disappeared at a disturbingly regular rate from national parks and forests across the United States and Canada for over a hundred years. Even though most of the cases can be accounted for as suicides, accidents, and even intentional disappearances, some of them are baffling both to relatives and the authorities. These are consistent with Native American stories coming from the same areas, especially from the Pacific Northwest, which tell of children and women disappearing and being suspected of having been carried off by hairy giants believed to be cannibals. This should bring to mind Tom's story of the man whose head was found in the Smoky Mountains after he went hunting for the monster said to live under a waterfall on Buck Creek.

Paulides pointed out the unusual behavior of blood-hounds/cadaver dogs involved in the search process for many of these disappearance victims. Sometimes when professionally trained search dogs picked up a scent trail, they would follow it only so far and then would cower and refuse to follow it further, as if it was left by something which terrified them. This fact is disturbingly consistent with Tom's experience with his dogs on his property and with Grover Krantz's observations about the terror with which dogs characteristically regard Bigfoot. The consistent canine reaction of abject horror to the creatures remains one of the best indications that a genuinely unknown animal of some kind is involved.

For decades, occasional stories surface from the Big Thicket country about hunters who disappear in the woods never to be found again. These include one case only a few years ago of two teenagers who went missing in the swamp near the Trinity River National Wildlife Preserve while squirrel hunting. It is presumed they somehow fell into the river and drowned and were swept away, but from what we have seen, they could have met with a far more terrifying fate that, without warning, transformed them from the hunters to the hunted.

The Seeahtiks and Renegade Cherokees

From his Cherokee ancestry and his knowledge of their shamanism and history in North Carolina, Tom began to suspect

Bigfoot connections to Native American tribes could be more direct than the Indians merely having knowledge of the hairy creatures. When the Cherokees were forcibly removed from their lands in the Smoky Mountains in the 1830s, some refused to go. They stayed behind and moved into the almost inaccessibly steep slopes of the mountains, adopting a primitive lifestyle both by choice and by the necessity of their rugged surroundings. In Tom's experience, some of these people may still be around:

> In the areas where the Bigfoot are seen up in these mountains, there could still be some rogue Cherokees who have lived in the wilderness dating back to the days of the Trail of Tears, when some refused to be removed by the whites. This could very well be one of the answers to the phenomena associated with the creatures. They could simply be Indians, or an even older race known to the Indians. It could quite simply be some Indians who prefer to live the way they do and have for thousands of years. Of course, that wouldn't account for their small size or lack of hairiness compared to the creatures, unless these Indians are masters of disguise or are able to do some kind of shapeshifting. But there is another possibility.
>
> The creatures could be remnants of, or maybe related to, the legendary Seeahtik tribe of the Pacific

Northwest. They are believed to be a race of hairy
giants seven to eight feet tall whose appearance is
like that of an animal covered with hair, like a bear.
Some native peoples of the Pacific Northwest believe
the Seeahtiks are not fully human and are an ancient
form of man. I have caught glimpses of Indians and
/or wild people here who look more human than
beast-like. I have found lean-tos, tent-like structures
similar to those used by the Cherokee, or perhaps
a primitive race of Neanderthal. The renegade
Cherokees might have chosen to live as primitively
as the hairy wild people.

The Seeahtiks were said by other tribes in the
Northwest to kill game by stunning their prey
with hypnotic powers and to be able to use psychic
ability to hide so well. They were also said to make
their homes in caves and to live underground. It all
sounds like it could be describing a Bigfoot. There is
another curious thing about them. They are said to
be able to speak and understand the ancient tongues
of the people indigenous to the Northwest.

I have been awakened in the night and heard
the Cherokee dialect being spoken outside of my
home in the mountains. Call it ghost sound or
whatever from the past, but I hardly think so.
Could it be that the creatures have had enough
contact with the Cherokees to understand their

language, and they sense me being part Cherokee and are trying to communicate with me?

I have learned enough to be wary and cautious when and where I travel here. If they choose to visit here and accept my gifts of food, fine. I will not venture into their camps. If I do, it's only by accident, especially if these creatures are anything like the Seeahtiks, because there was one other trait the Indians believe they had—they were cannibals.

The cannibal stories you hear become far too real when you hear banging in the brush in the cold dead of winter, knowing they are searching for any game to eat. It all becomes frightfully real. Your biggest fear of being eaten becomes reality for a second or two. This is not exactly the most fun hobby in the world. Why I continue is a mystery, too.

I remember them or something eating my dogs and finding pieces of what was left of them in the woods. I remember the ear-piercing screams of the creature when I knew he was stealing my puppy as it ran off into the dark woods behind my house, leaving me never to see my dog again. If that is not enough to make your heart skip a beat, I don't know what is.

Giant "Without Moccasins" Indians

The Karankawas, a historic but long forgotten tribe of Indians of imposing physical stature might be involved in at least some of the wild man sightings in Southeast Texas, similar to how the Seeahtiks in the Northwest and what Tom suspects could be unknown Indians in the Smoky Mountains could be involved in Bigfoot sightings. According to authorities cited in the Texas History Association Handbook, the Karankawas lived along the coast of the Gulf of Mexico from Corpus Christi Bay to Galveston Bay and inland to the mouth of the Trinity River at the Big Thicket's southwestern edge. They traveled between the various islands, bays, bayous, swamps, rivers, and tributaries in crude dugout canoes hewn from large trees.

They were completely eliminated from the historical record and were thought to have been extirpated as early as the 1850s from exposure to diseases introduced by European settlers and from fighting other indigenous peoples and the whites. Much of what is known about them is legendary or apocryphal, but they are said to have had some traits which, from what we have considered thus far in this book, should seem strikingly familiar.

The males averaged over six feet in height with some approaching seven feet. They lived a barely human, hunter/gatherer, subsistence lifestyle, and had an overall appearance that was so primitive that some authorities think they might actually have been survivors of the prehistoric Abilene Man, or possibly hybrids between that species and modern homo sapiens. Their faces and torsos were heavily tattooed, and with their waist-length, black hair hanging over their shoulders, they had a fearsome and repugnant appearance to their enemies. The neighboring Tonkawas called them the "bare-footed," or "without moccasins," tribe. The mere sight of their huge footprints and the sound of their prolonged, loud, animal-like howl struck fear in the hearts of their enemies.

They went about scantily attired in loincloths, except in cold weather when they would wear animal skins. In the summer, they covered themselves with alligator grease and mud to repel mosquitoes. Their resultant stench evoked horror and was a sure giveaway to those who opposed them that an attack from the Karankawas was at hand.

Although they didn't regard human flesh as a regular food source, evidence suggests the Karankawas did practice ceremonial cannibalism. They would tie up a horrified captive, and dancing maniacally around the stake, they would dart in, slice off a piece of flesh with a sharp blade, and roast it in front of the victim. Then they would devour it, as the victim witnessed his own slow death.

The large bare feet, the awful stench, the near-gigantic physical proportions, and the terrifyingly loud howl are identical to descriptions of the wild man, but what of the hairy body that is always attributed to Bigfoot? Imagine if you were to have a close encounter and catch a fleeting glance of a Karankawa warrior or shaman in the dim, scattered light of dense thicket woods.

You might just have been overcome and disoriented by his intense body odor and had your nerves frayed from his high-decibel howl. The combination of his towering height, tattooed torso, mud-smeared body, his wearing of animal skins and his long shaggy hair could easily give a startled witness the impression he was completely covered with hair.

Is this, then, the fearsome, cannibalistic, ancient form of man of which Native American legends speak? The similarities are so striking some researchers have speculated whether the Karankawas didn't disappear from Texas and make their way to the Pacific Northwest in sufficient numbers to sustain their population until the present day. Although, we cannot completely discount the possibility that this could account for some sightings, the creature in Tom's photo is clearly more likely to be a completely hair-covered primate than a human being wearing animal skins.

We are forced to concede the likelihood that sightings of both wild, hairy hominids and survivors of an unknown, ancient, non-homo sapien forms of man have been happening probably since the unrecorded past continuing to the present day. There could be reasons the two different types of sightings tend to occur in the same geographic areas. They could both be attracted to the energetic conditions indicated by the recurrent presence of the mystery light-forms, and there could also be a shamanic connection.

It has already been noted that in some Native American traditions, Bigfoot is regarded as a spirit being capable of physical manifestation. It is thus considered a guardian of places of special power that potentially are gateways to the spirit world or land of the ancestors—and to act as an ally to tribal shamans, assisting them in gaining access to that world. Along with the Karankawas' warriors, their shamans might have also intentionally imitated the wild man's behavior and appearance in hopes of being magically imbued with the mysterious creature's powers.

At least two different kinds of sightings, then, seem to be happening involving wild, hairy hominid entities, one more human-like, and one more ape-like—a point which brings up an interesting question. If there really are surviving remnants of the Seeahtik, Karankawas, or other primitive tribes, what kind of incidents might they produce that are distinctive of more typical Bigfoot sightings? One type is obviously the kind of disappearances from national parks that Paulides writes about. As difficult as it is to entertain such possibilities, a handful of stories reported to Rob also suggest involvement by Indians not known to still exist.

Rick, a professional treasure hunter from the Beaumont, Texas area, told Rob about what happened to him in the Trinity River swamp on the Big Thicket's western edge in the mid-1980s. He was planning to go to a specific spot, which an airplane flyover magnetometer reading had indicated a significant magnetic anomaly that could be made by a large metal deposit. He was hoping to find some of the legendary pirate Jean Lafitte's treasure, which was rumored to have been buried near the river at the mouth of Trinity Bay a hundred and fifty years ago.

Before Rick could get back into the swamp, he was stopped by a Texas game warden who advised him to go no further. There had been several recent incidences of hunters having been attacked by bow and arrow, and the game warden himself had narrowly escaped being hit. He described his assailant as big, practically naked, and dark-skinned. The only explanation the game warden had for the yet-to-be-apprehended suspects involved is they were a bunch of survivalist weirdos playing wild Indian.

This would be a reasonable assumption, Rick said, but he wondered why they would be attacking hunters with bows and arrows when they should know they might receive return fire from high-powered deer rifles. The game warden said he wondered the same thing, but noted something about the arrow shot at him, which he managed to retrieve, that made the incident even more bizarre. He had examined it closely, and it was not a metal-tipped arrow of modern manufacture. It looked like a genuine handmade artifact using two-hundred-year-old technology.

Its appearance could only be described as primitive, which was the also the word that best described his attacker. He said there was something very strange about the alleged Indian. His appearance seemed so primitive as to be out of place in our time. What made this account compelling to Rob, even though it was a third-hand story, was it corroborated a couple of other stories he had received from the same area.

The owner of a remote fish camp and bait shop off the lower Trinity River near the mouth of Trinity Bay had been told by an electrical utility lineman of his sighting of a small band of practically naked, wild Indians who appeared primitive. When the fish camp owner went to investigate the matter for himself, he was quickly discouraged from continuing his search by a gruesome and horrifying discovery. He found what was left of a human skeleton strapped to a tree not far from where the lineman had seen the Indians. This scene sounds strikingly like the remnants of a Karankawa ritualistic cannibalism ceremony.

One other intriguing story could place surviving Karankawas in the Big Thicket. A lady from Saratoga told Rob some of her family members had gone hunting somewhere along the Little Pine Island Bayou. They had just come around a bend that opened up an unobstructed view for a good distance when they were shocked to see a large, almost naked Indian in a rough-hewn dugout boat. What impressed them most, and is consistent with the other stories, was the Indian's extremely primitive appearance.

Probably the bewilderment of seeing something so out-of-place and out-of-time, or maybe an extreme sense of high strangeness, spooked the hunters, who beat a hasty retreat and made no effort to investigate. Their description of the incident, however, could not better describe the Karankawas, who were known to fish the coastal waters of the area from their rough-hewn pirogue boats.

All of these reputed incidents, by the way, happened within no more than a few miles of where the two squirrel-hunting teenage boys mentioned earlier mysteriously disappeared only a few years ago. Their disappearance might not only be linked with these other suspicious activities, but it would place such bizarre goings-on well within the present day time frame.

Clearly, the wild man/Bigfoot sightings, at least in some cases, cannot be taken as cases of mistaken identity of what are actually ancient Indians, or prehistoric forms of man. There seem to be two distinctly different types of sightings. The overlaps and similarities of the two are intriguing and raise many as yet unanswered questions.

Are the Mysterious Lights Actually the Creatures in Another Form?

To his amazement, when Tom set up motion-sensitive game trail cameras to photograph what he thought might be Bigfoot-type animals that had been killing his beloved dogs, he got pictures of strange balls of light instead. It was then he began to suspect these lights were related to the well-known Brown Mountain ghost lights, which are seen only a couple of valleys over from Tom's land, and to similar lights he frequently witnessed on the mountain slopes where he lived. The following summarizes what Tom feels he has been forced to consider as the possible significance of the lights:

Typical of Native American belief, as was explained to me by Choctaw medicine woman, Khat Hansen, is that what are called ghost lights, in some cases at least, are the intermediary phase of Bigfoot moving from the spirit world to this reality or vice versa. In other words, the ghost lights are the Bigfoot. As fantastic as that sounds, it is consistent with what my cameras could be showing and to the eyewitness account reported to Rob that claimed to have actually witnessed Bigfoot materializing out of a luminous fog on Bragg Road in the Big Thicket.

The ability to transform itself into a ball of light might not be limited to the Bigfoot. Native American traditions of the Choctaw and Yaqui, for example, claim there are shamans who have developed that power. Rob's research found that the same is rumored among the Cajuns in south Louisiana to be true of voodoo practitioners who can shape shift into the Rougarou, a Bigfoot-type hairy creature, and the fifolet, a bright ball of light.

Similar abilities are attributed to the "flying men" cult in Haiti as was discussed in detail in Rob's first book. They are said to be able to travel long distances by somehow utilizing the magical arts to change their bodies into spheres of light, then upon arrival at their destinations, to return into their original physical bodies.

When you start talking about mysterious lights, the door is opened for speculations on UFOs, nature spirits, wormholes in nature, and unusual magnetic fields, as well as ancient forms of man, sorcerers of black magic and voodoo priests. Too many variables at once make it hard for a normal mind to comprehend. When I first started this work, I never believed I was looking for something that could be a little bit supernatural. I was only after an ape or some kind of human being that chose to live in the forest or remote mountain regions, but the more time I put into this the more complex and mysterious it all becomes.

These Ancient Ones seem to know how to elude capture or detection by using this field of mysterious energy to cross over into some kind of other world, possibly by means of something like a wormhole. The wormholes transport them to safety at the blink of an eye. If you see a Bigfoot, it's because they want you to, not because you have worked hard to find one. Some practitioners of the Black Arts are said to know how to summon this energy from the earth and utilize it for their own interests, the same way the Ancient Hairy Ones do. When you look at things from this angle, it's a little easier to accept. The Unknown becomes a bit known. Many of the lights may be the Ancient Ones traveling, Indian shamans traveling, and/or spirit energy trying to reveal itself for reasons unknown.

The monster always stays just far enough away to leave room for doubt as to what it really is, which could be a sign of fear, intelligence, good instincts to leave human beings alone, or a combination of all the above.

I sort of believe there very well could be a passageway of some sort near my home to another world underground in these mountains. There could be life forms we know little about, which exist inside the earth and for whatever reason sometimes come to the exterior, perhaps to intervene in the affairs of men. This is part theory and a bit of my imagination at work, but from what I've experienced, anything is possible at this point. To close one's mind would be foolish. I will continue this work, regardless of the obstacles. I am beginning to think what the Indians say is true, that the creatures very well could be a type of spirit people with powers way beyond ours. Too much has happened for there not to be some kind of a supernatural or paranormal part to this mystery as well.

We are fully aware of the major concerns of opening Pandora's Box by allowing paranormal aspects into consideration of the nature of Bigfoot and the ghost lights. We are, however, emphatically not interested in simply giving readers our assurances about these matters, as if we were claiming they come from a revelatory source or that we have access to some kind of secret insider information.

The inherently subjective nature of following the lead of indigenous peoples and our European ancestors by employing intuitive methods of inquiry, however, does allow for paranormal aspects to enter into mystery hominid research. It does muddy the waters. As we both have been forced to conclude from our own respective experiences and observations in the field, however, considerations of these strange energy and light factors, including the possibility that at least some of the lights might actually *be* Bigfoot, must be included if the phenomenon is to be seriously studied in its entirety.

Some of Tom's photographs of mysterious light-forms that suggest this might be the case are also featured on our website. One photo shows distinct animal-like features beginning to take shape in a light-form. This could be an example of an unknown animal materializing from a luminous energy field in the same way Bigfoot purportedly does. When viewing the photo, note that the game trail camera was placed three feet off the ground, so this would have to have been a fairly large animal.

TEN

Where Do We Go from Here?

Rob and Billy Visit Tom

In July of 2012, after almost three years of corresponding by e-mails and phone calls, it was high time for me to meet Tom face-to-face and personally check out the area where there has been so much Bigfoot activity. Although it's almost a thousand miles from the Big Thicket to the Blue Ridge Parkway, I decided to drive so I would would not have to depend on Tom to ferry me around. Joining me on the trip was a friend I have known since our elementary school days in Sour Lake, whom we will call Billy to protect his identity. Billy lives in an old fishing camp right across the Neches River from a swamp that is part of the Big Thicket National Preserve.

I had lost contact with Billy for almost thirty years, when a few years ago I got an e-mail from him. He had become intensely interested in Bigfoot research over the years and was an active, insightful blogger on several Bigfoot research sites, which is where he learned of my book. He was surprised I had published a book on the subject, but not surprised that I had been exposed to the Big Thicket wild man stories. He'd had his own experiences with the big shaggy beast.

One night when he was just a kid, the thing apparently sneaked in under the cover of darkness and thick woods down the bayou and into the outskirts of Sour Lake. It was probably foraging for fruit that had just ripened in local fig trees, one of which was in Billy's backyard. Billy got up to get a drink and heard a disturbance. He pulled up the window shade and was horrified to find the monster staring at him through his bedroom window. As was typical of the times, nobody talked about those things from fear of ridicule, so Billy and I never knew about each other's disturbing experiences until over fifty years later. It was reassuring that he was willing to come out and talk about it, and it confirmed my suspicions there were more sightings of the wild man than one would expect.

After making that contact, we made several forays into the Preserve and the Angelina National Forest looking for Bigfoot evidence. Billy took an interest in Tom's work and they began their own correspondence, so he was eager to make the trip and meet Tom. The following is Tom's brief account of our visit:

I had long anticipated the visit of both of my friends. They arrived with gear in hand ready to rumble and to share a week with me. I was very glad to meet them. Both of them being East Texas boys growing up in the swamps, with their backgrounds they would enlighten me on some things I had experienced and give me a new inner strength I never knew I had.

Their first night here in the mountains was spent in a motel room. They were very tired from the long trip and not so sure exactly where my Bigfoot cabin was. I was so eager to share stories with them. During the second day Rob and Billy gathered firewood for our ceremony to attract the creatures in front of my cabin for when I got off work and was able to join them. We all agreed the best way to attract the creatures was to build a fire, eat some food, and just be cool and laid back. The Bigfoot are attracted to speech and we knew that. We all thought they would come, and they did. We heard the loud banging noises they made in the woods and took it as their acknowledgment of us.

We all told our stories. Rob looked at me and said, "Tom, do you realize what is going on here?" He gently pushed his horn-rimmed glasses from the tip of his nose to eye level and said, "The tree bent over in a curved manner on the road coming in, and the tree bent here at this cabin mean a lot. Notice that none of the trees around them are bent like this, so it's not like the wind or some natural force bent them. If you think about it, something with enormous strength would have to have done it."

Then Billy said, "Tom, this means the Bigfoot and/or spirits own this place as much as you own it. They consider it their territory and just don't know exactly what to do with you."

Rob replied, "Tom, all three of us have considerable Native American heritage. Our Indian ancestors believed that sometimes the spirit beings from another dimension choose people who are sensitive to interact with this material world and their spirit world, sort of like an intermediary between the two. In the old days this was the responsibility of the shamans. I believe this might be your case here as well."

I was a bit dumbfounded and did not believe I was really a shaman, but whose perception of what is real in this world or the spirit world is right? It's all up to interpretation. What a man believes he is in his heart—he is.

The last night we got together Rob and Billy had already started the glowing campfire when I arrived. The moon was full and it seemed to dance

through the trees. We could see well into the woods
that night. We talked about all the variables in the
puzzle: moving lights with faces, shapeshifting,
renegade Cherokees still living in the mountains,
noises and sounds that seem to come from nowhere,
human footprints, ape footprints, and my pictures
of faces that look so human, but ape-like as well.

All of us had our assumptions, perceptions, and beliefs,
but really we knew nothing for sure. What I did know based
on my experiences was there was a viable breeding population of some type of primate or perhaps an ancient form
of man on my land, and that was it. I found a skull on my
land of what I believe was a baby Bigfoot back in the summer of 2000, so that indicated they were physically real and
not just a spirit. The photo I have of the large ape gives even
more credence to my many encounters. Rob and I have collected enough evidence to at least prove we are not just making this stuff up. There is evidence of a largely invisible world
here and the rest of society only has a small idea of what is
really going on here. We all agreed the Bigfoot have enough
sense to keep avoiding humans for their own protection.
Billy and Rob suggested we leave some semiprecious stones
from the local mountains as gifts to the creatures to see what
their reaction would be. The outcome of this is too early to tell,
but I will continue to leave them stones with my gifts of food.

My two friends left to go back to Texas on July 6. I eagerly await Rob's return to the mountains to continue our work together, and hope he has some luck down in the swamps in the meantime.

Tom's Updates after Rob's and Billy's Visit

A couple from Charlotte said they wanted to rent my cabin. They had three months' rent in advance, so I rented it to them on November 1, 2012, despite their looks. He was covered in tattoos, and so was she. She had more nose and body piercing than him and they both looked wild to me. I did not care, because I needed the money. I warned them about all the noises they would hear at night and told them it was just bears, so not to worry. I was afraid they would leave if I told them about Bigfoot, so I kept my mouth shut.

A few days later early one morning, they called me from town and said they were leaving and wanted their deposit back. So I met them in town and asked them a few questions. Why were they leaving in such a hurry when they would lose two months of rent? They said at night they heard helicopter-type sounds, like blades churning around the cabin, and frequently saw lights go through the forest at night. They also heard loud bangs on trees, which frightened them. They had left almost all their clothes, all their belongings, food, beer, sheets, and more for me to do with as I pleased. I returned their money and wished them well.

A few months earlier, I had rented the cabin to a pack of young adults whose idea of a good time was a bag of weed, some beer, and whatever sex they could round up. One day I found the cabin vacant and all of their stuff was still there. They paid the rent two months in advance but left suddenly. I had to talk to one of their associates to find out what happened.

Their friend told me the boys were smoking a doobie when they heard the monster outside. One boy grabbed his pistol and went outside only to see a shadowy form in the dark. He hollered out loud and the creature screamed. The boy dropped the gun and ran. The other two boys picked him up on the road on his way back to town. To this day the boys have never returned to claim their clothing and furniture—they were scared shitless. I don't blame them.

If this keeps up, I never will be able to rent out this cabin for any length of time. So, Rob and I have decided to name it our Bigfoot Research Center.

I have slept in the cabin a few times since Rob's and Billy's visit simply because I like the area. I have a nice house to sleep in on the mountain, but sometimes prefer the night air there by the creek, and besides that I usually build a fire and eat some good grilled food. It has always been a hot spot for the Bigfoot. They eat the frogs out of the creek here. It's a priority to them as a feeding spot. I left a fifty-pound sack of dog food here for my dogs, but something mysteriously got the food a week earlier. A bear would have made a mess eating the food—but something carried it away. I tried to forget about the dog food–stealing varmint so I could enjoy the evening. I had just got ready to bunk down for the night when I heard a limb snap in the back corner of the yard. Not having a real good feeling, I shut the windows to the cabin. I was scared.

About an hour into my sleep I was awakened by the couch moving on the porch outside where the dogs usually slept. The dogs were growling and something was chasing them in the yard. I looked outside reluctantly to see a pair of red eyes glowing with a huge black form behind them. The dogs ran across the creek and the form remained. The growling from the dogs soon changed to howling. They were scared and so was I.

The next thing I heard was the couch being thrown into the side of the cabin. Now I was really scared, about to flip out. I wondered if the front door would be ripped off and me left to fend for my life. But luckily when daylight came, I ventured outside to see the couch torn in half and most of it dragged into the yard. There was no way bears or human beings could have done what was done with that couch. I figured the Bigfoot came back to look for food, found none and threw my couch in pieces out of anger, or they just plain wanted me out. This was not the first time I had been run out of this area.

EPILOGUE:
A Model for Future Bigfoot/Mystery Hominid Research

We don't claim to have all the answers to the Bigfoot enigma. In fact, the results of our research and experiences in the field have been humbling for both of us. In many ways our efforts have yielded more questions than answers, the central question being: Given the multitude of reputable sightings and other data that point to the reality of Bigfoot's existence, how do they remain essentially hidden from humankind? We are convinced any serious approach to answering that question needs to take all the elements of Bigfoot encounters into account.

Virtually all current Bigfoot research groups and individuals assume Bigfoot is no more than an undiscovered great ape. In our opinion, this model of research amounts to not playing with a full deck and will always yield inconclusive results. Bigfoot will not be found in any substantive way, nor will contact with the creatures be made for any prolonged period of time, if this assumption continues to be the basis of research methods.

We have both observed in our respective field research and by photographs taken by each of us independently that Bigfoot appearances are often accompanied by electromagnetic disturbances, sometimes including unknown lightforms. These phenomena have been remarked on by a few investigators, but it has led them to conclude Bigfoot sightings constitute some kind of phantom phenomenon. Because of our views on this matter, we are largely dismissed as cranks by organized Bigfoot research groups and are no longer invited to participate with them or attend their conferences. This is a shame in many ways, because we have more in common with them than they are likely to think.

Both of us firmly believe the creatures have a solid, flesh-and-blood existence. The weird energy manifestations associated with them, however, might give them unusual camouflaging ability, which they use both to stalk prey and to elude detection by humans. This camouflaging might extend to mind-to-mind or telepathic communication, with which they could hide in the blind spots of humans, thus rendering them virtually invisible in their natural environment.

Because of what can only be called their psychic ability, the Bigfoot are keenly sensitive to human intentionality. For this reason it is important to abandon the counterproductive, quasi-military, invade-and-conquer attitude that dominates current research. All this does is alert the creatures to potential danger and provoke them to hide. Instead, we hope to gain their trust. We will try to develop long-term contact with a small, stable population of the creatures that will enable us to get enough quality photographs and video footage to constitute conclusive proof of their existence. Hopefully, this will be only the first step in our beginning to understand these splendid creatures.

This will require us to pick out a few specific locations and stay put in them for prolonged periods, not flitter around from one place to another after staying at each for only a few days. The most productive areas potentially will be places where there is a long, established tradition of sightings and a concurrent history of unusual electromagnetic anomalies, such as ghost lights or other mystery luminous phenomena. There are certain spots in the Big Thicket National Preserve in Texas that fit this description. We invite our readers to suggest other promising spots, but for the time being we will focus on Tom's land in the mountains of western North Carolina.

The great advantage for future research on Tom's property is that it abuts many hundreds of thousands of acres of national forest. The Bigfoot groups who live there seem to be fairly stationary—Tom has heard and observed them at different times through the years. In other words, they do not seem to migrate, but generally stay in the area for food, suitable habitat, and shelter.

In addition, the area behind Tom's property is a bear sanctuary where no hunting is allowed except for limited seasons regulated by the Forest Service. We will not have to hunt far for the creatures. There is substantial evidence they maintain a presence on this and adjoining land in Pisgah National Forest and the Blue Ridge Parkway. Another advantage is no one can access the government sanctuary without Tom's permission, because the road to it runs through his land. It is his private property and he also owns the easement.

Putting out food for wildlife is not permitted on government land, but because Tom is a landowner, he legally can put out whatever foods he chooses to attract the Bigfoot onto his property. He has done just that for decades. Over the years he has found they are omnivorous and will pretty much eat anything. By providing food, which they sometimes gratefully acknowledge by leaving him gifts like feathers and acorns, Tom has gone a long way toward winning their trust. We vow to never break that trust. In all our research efforts we will use an approach that extends kindness toward the hairy wild people.

We are fully aware we are not likely to be successful by limiting this to a one- or two-man project. For that reason, we invite our readers to join us. Members of academic or scientific institutions who are not afraid of risking their reputations and those with professional photographic or video crew experience would be of particular interest, but up to a certain point anyone who meets our qualifications is welcome. Keep in mind, though, we are not looking for converts or true believers who take every owl hoot, distant coyote howl or breaking twig in the dark to be a sign Bigfoot has showed up. An open mind tempered with a healthy dose of skepticism is more useful.

Anyone who makes an investment of expertise, time or funds into this project, however, must remember this. Despite how promising our chances look, there are no guarantees our efforts will produce anything conclusive. Much of this work is pure drudgery. Patience and dedication will be at a premium. This is not something we human beings like to think about, but in this case, we just might not be in control of the situation. If they choose to respond to our entreaties and establish some kind of meaningful communication with us, it will likely be their decision, not ours.

The following is Tom's full description of how he was able to use a hidden game trail camera to get the photo of what appears to be a Bigfoot or an unknown hairy, black quadruped featured in this book. This came after years of failed attempts and only when Tom used some trickery.

On September 15, 2010, I got the best Bigfoot picture bar none in the world. I was running two game cams one hundred yards from my house, one facing south, the other due north. The creature had noticed my south-facing camera and turned it upside down. It had been loosely chained to a small pine tree and laid up against a tree. He simply found it and turned it face down in the dirt. When he turned around, my north facing camera got him. He has a bewildered look on his face and appears to be staring right at the camera.

The same day I got the picture, the highway crew working on the road below my house told me they saw the creature run across the road in front of where they were working.

I suspect with the half-hard penis he has in my photo it's mating season and he is running a rut marking his territory similar to how deer do. With his well-endowed equipment he could easily pole vault through the rhododendrons and brush and continue his journey with ease. He appears healthy, hairy, and looks quite virile.

Now the biggest challenge is to figure out what to do with the photo. I have had some time to ponder this riddle.

In order for me to get this photo, I spent two plus years of my life changing batteries, relocating equipment several times, and had to fool the Bigfoot with two hidden cameras. It's like trying to be a spy on a would-be friend, so you can help him, not hurt him.

There will still be scoffers. But who cares? They can kiss my fanny. It's me doing all the work. To be successful you need resources, knowledge, an open mind and try to make good observations based on the information coming your way.

Not too many people will do this work for six months, much less on and off since 1991. That's over twenty years.

In the past, I used high-powered cameras and hiked into their territory only to be run out, mock attacked, and made to be much afraid of getting too close to their nest or hive. I invited them to me on my turf this time, and it worked. However, they seem to know what cameras are and usually try to avoid them at all costs.

I have clearly made friends with them or they would never have allowed me to get the picture I now have. In the past they would tear up my equipment, but not this time. I think they consider me to be part of their clan because of my looking after them and they're trying to help me all they can in their own way.

My experiences with the wild man or Sasquatch are far too bizarre to have been made up. I will subject myself to a lie detector on national TV if somebody would request it. That's how much I believe in what I've done and what I have been exposed to.

APPENDIX:

Questionable Evidence,
Questionable People

At the time of this writing, it came out in the news that Dr. Melba Ketchum, a Texas veterinarian, claimed she had DNA evidence that proves the existence of Bigfoot. This is Tom's account of his dealings with her some years prior to her announcement:

> Several years ago, I found a skull in the woods near my house. It was strange looking so I found a place I could send it to for testing in Timpson, Texas, called DNA Diagnostics under the care of Melba Ketchum. I sent the skull, and shortly

after I sent the skull, I noticed that Dr. Ketchum had suddenly gotten into the Bigfoot business. She bragged she had in her possession a baby Sasquatch skull and it was undergoing analysis.

Over the next three years, I approached her and her technicians and had a few conversations with her personally on the phone after fifty-some odd attempts at calls, mostly to be put off and so forth. She pretty much told me crazy stuff like, "You already had your chance with the skull, it's my turn now," and, "Rome was not built in a day." After three years, she never told me what I had, so I demanded my skull back and she sent it to me and kept my money.

The people I have met in this business are self-centered egotistical clowns. Even the doctors will use people for their own benefit. When I got the skull back, I sent it to Canada thinking I might get out of the politics in America, and boy was I wrong. I sent it to Paleo-DNA lab in Thunder Bay, Ontario. The first day the examiner called and told me excitedly, "Mr. Burnette, you have a high-level primate as far as we can tell. It was not at all what we had expected."

I was ecstatic but only for seven days. After seven days the examiner called and said, "Mr. Burnette, you have a deer skull." I reminded him of his first statement of a primate and he replied, "Tom, you did have a primate, but now you have a deer skull."

I was ticked at the least, I demanded my skull back and again called Dr. Ketchum's office in Texas, talking to a young technician in the lab. I will not use any names to protect these people, anyway none have done me any favors. The technician told me to resend part of the skull, so I sawed out a piece of the inner skull and sent it again for the second time. After he received it he called, and told me I had some human mitochondria in the cranium tissue. He explained that the same thing for a chimp would light up as human and or apes as well. The next day he was gone. I never talked to him again and was never able to talk again to Melba Ketchum.

To this day they still have my DNA sample. The kind of people you meet in this business are all glory hounds who will do anything to put a feather in their cap. Really what's the big deal with this Bigfoot thing? The Indians have been aware of them for hundreds of years—there is nothing to discover. Most of them recognize Bigfoot as a different kind of human being, with animal-like characteristics, who avoid humans mostly at all costs. One thing Rob Riggs and I have both learned is change comes slow and with tiresome workloads, especially for those of us who do want to make a difference.

Again, I want to emphasize that we are not completely sure what we have. It could be some weird kind of animal, or it could be a Bigfoot baby skull. We do not care at this point. The fact remains that I have been told twice by two different people that I had a skull with DNA that resembled human mitochondria by two different sources. The lab in Canada told me the same thing before they changed their story and called it a deer skull.

The credibility of Ketchum's office is even far worse. Her technician took it on himself to divulge the facts to me after I told him I was unhappy with the way I was treated, so I sent it twice, the second time only a small piece. Then he told me what I had. The next day he was gone, probably fired for telling the truth.

I would like to say we are asking for help from someone who has experience to check part of our skull for another independent test outside of government bureaucracy, and those who are after self-glorification. Our only objective is to help the Bigfoot by providing access areas where they can live off limits to others who could cause them some discomfort by hunting on, or approaching their sacred grounds where they live and forage for food.

Regardless of the outcome of this study we feel like with the photos we have obtained there is enough photographic evidence to warrant more study. So in a nutshell we are not expecting anything from another DNA study, but if it something comes out positive that would be great. It might wind up really being just another animal.

Out of common decency, Ketchum's office should have told me at least what the truth was. There are numerous complaints about how they operate and other researchers like myself and Rob Riggs have been shanghaied by these people. We very optimistically look to tomorrow.

Tom's Concluding Thoughts

Even with as much as I've been through at this point, I still really can't be sure what the hell they are. I can only speculate, even though I've seen them and photographed them. I can't just go ask somebody, because not even a doctor of zoology can tell you anything. No one has a working model of a skeletal system, so scientists who want to be politically correct prefer to believe they do not exist—but believe me—they do.

My lady friend complains about me being a madman who sees a different world up here in the mountains—full of wild Indians and strange creatures which appear to fit another time, lost apparently to our modern world. Some of what I see here doesn't fit the 2010s, but perhaps other times and dimensions overlap here in this strange area.

Maybe there could be wormholes of some kind that occur in nature and connect us to parallel worlds and universes.

That could be why some things just don't seem to fit. Time and space interwoven and strewn through this strange electromagnetic energy seems to be more apparent in some places than others. There is a place close by where you can take a picture of a human being and the person appears sideways or you don't recognize them at all; their features are warped.

If it's not the energy or a parallel world, another explanation might be Stone Age Indian Neanderthals who continue to exist in heavily forested steep areas, which are almost inaccessible to normal lazy modern humans. They could exist almost invisibly because of the extreme terrain, and there's 500,000 acres of that behind my house. All of it is steep, all the way to Linville Gorge, Linville Falls, Mount Mitchell, Blue Ridge Parkway, on to Pisgah, and it continues into Cherokee. I have seen signs of these people and/or animals in all these places.

There are hundreds, perhaps thousands, of reports of unknown animals every year. Who knows really what the figure is, because only a small amount of folks might actually report anything at all. They are reluctant from fear of not being believed. Yet there are no efforts to help these unknown creatures who exist beside us. There is quite simply much we don't understand. Despite our modern world, there are many things in nature we have no grasp of at all.

I am convinced there are other dimensions that overlap ours. I am beginning to believe some of my encounters are with nature spirits from another part of this world. There are so many things that point in that direction. I need to keep it simple, but none of this is simple because it makes no rational sense.

We continue to make fascinating discoveries in the depths of the oceans, life forms stranger and stranger. As we reach out into the wilderness looking for new life forms and as our technology increases, our discoveries will increase both in the wilderness and in the inner earth as well. We will soon find there are things that really do go bump in the night. The discoveries we make in the next century will amaze and baffle us, if we don't destroy our Garden of Eden in the meantime. I pray not, both for us and the ape-man.

I personally believe them to be a subhuman species, intelligent like us, but preferring a mere hand-to-mouth existence. I also believe that because of urbanization, there are only small groups of this important species of man left in pockets of dense forestland, which are fewer every year because of forestry practices such as clear-cutting. Because of this unrelenting, never-ending change of our ecological world, this wonder of nature, the ape-man will eventually lose its habitat. And with the loss of its natural habitat, it will have no home, no food, and no woods to live in. It will be gone forever. The fate that awaits the ape-man could be ours as well. It's up to us. There is still a little time. We must believe in tomorrow.

Rob's Concluding Thoughts

The increase in purported Bigfoot sightings within the last decade, and the growing widespread acceptance of there being even a remote possibility of another species of advanced primate living on this planet, has led me to think optimistically that we might be headed toward some kind of expansion of awareness. I am often told by well-intentioned people that they don't want Bigfoot to be discovered because they want the mystery to stay alive. The only way the mystery would die is if the creatures were proven to be no more than a previously unknown but perfectly normal animal. As I hope the reader has seen by now—there is far more to the Bigfoot enigma than that.

Contact with the Hairy Ones wouldn't kill our sense of mystery, rather it would deepen our awe of both the wonders of nature and of ourselves. Hopefully, it would heal us of that great sickness of the modern materialistic age which defines and limits us to our bodily existence, and would restore in us the sense of wonder with which our ancestors experienced the Great Sacred Mystery at the core of our being. We would then find that not only is Bigfoot a mysterious being, and not just an unknown animal, but we are also mysterious beings, and not just physical entities.

Normally, human beings can journey in spirit form only to the reality that lies beyond the one limited to our five senses. For native peoples it is precisely its ability to *bodily* live in and move between the two worlds that makes the

Bigfoot so significant to them. The physical presence of the mysterious beasts might have served as an indicator to ancient peoples that any energy fields they encounter in the vicinity of where the creatures and the mystery light-forms appear could serve as an aid to their objectively entering the spirit world. It would indicate that the energy in question was not just a random unknown force producing subjective hallucinations, but was a gateway to the land of the ancestors.

It is an accepted fact that temples and monumental structures were erected on sacred sites where the ancients encountered founts of the mysterious energy in question. Notre Dame and Canterbury are among the cathedrals in medieval Europe which were built on the remains of those earlier edifices. They both contain art depicting what was called the Woodwose or Wild Man of the Woods. Could this be a dim reminder of a former time when our remote European ancestors also recognized the role of the Hairy Ones as guardians of places of potentially consciousness-transforming sacred energy?

This might help explain what some Native American shamans mean when they refer to Bigfoot as guardians of the gateways to the spirit world or portals of higher consciousness. Even though people still catch glimpses of them, this role of the hairy wild people has been all but forgotten. If we are lucky, it might be restored.

To Write to the Authors

If you wish to contact the author or would like more information about this book, please write to the author in care of Llewellyn Worldwide, and we will forward your request. Both the author and publisher appreciate hearing from you and learning of your enjoyment of this book and how it has helped you. Llewellyn Worldwide cannot guarantee that every letter written to the author can be answered, but all will be forwarded. Please write to:

Tom Burnette & Rob Riggs
⁒ Llewellyn Worldwide
2143 Wooddale Drive
Woodbury, MN 55125-2989

Please enclose a self-addressed stamped envelope for reply, or $1.00 to cover costs. If outside the USA, enclose an international postal reply coupon.